MANNERS MATTER

for STUDENTS

MANNERS MATTER

for STUDENTS

FRED HARTLEY
ANDREA HARTLEY SMITH

BARBOUR
PUBLISHING

Cover image © Wes Youssi, The DesignWorks Group, Inc.
www.thedesignworksgroup.com

Published by Barbour Publishing, Inc., P.O. Box 719, Uhrichsville, Ohio 44683, www.barbourbooks.com

Our mission is to publish and distribute inspirational products offering exceptional value and biblical encouragement to the masses.

 Member of the
Evangelical Christian
Publishers Association

Printed in the United States of America

5 4 3 2 1

To my two beautiful, young daughters:
Lily Anne and Georgia Grace who
have yet to figure out exactly
why Manners Matter.

contents

introduction

"Manners for students?
You've got to be kidding!"

Are manners really meant for teenagers? Absolutely! Do manners apply to a generation that has grown to value individuality—being different from everyone else? Yes, now more than ever!

Manners are timeless. Manners are valuable. Manners are necessary in today's world to help us become all that we were created by God to be.

This is not your average manners book. It is not written for all audiences. It is written specifically for students who want to live confidently and respectfully toward others and to be shown respect in return. We all want that!

This book will help you discover—and perhaps rediscover—new things about life, about yourself, and about others around you.

For example:

Have you ever been at the dinner table and took a bite of something you absolutely could not swallow? What do you do in this situation?

This is only a small, momentary problem that will not make or break us, but if we don't know how to act in these small moments, they could cause us unnecessary embarrassment.

How about a much deeper problem?

What if you are caught standing in front of a group of people with nothing to say? How are you to act in a situation like this?

How you react can shape your personality—perhaps even your future. That is why manners are so important. We need them to be able to live with poise and purpose. Reading this book will help you

- build confidence in your interactions with people;
- be at ease in new settings;
- feel better about yourself;
- avoid embarrassing situations;
- make friends easily;
- become a leader and an example for others; and
- be courteous toward others.

Those are big promises, but you'll soon discover that manners are like chocolate chip cookies—you can live without them, but they sure make life happier and more enjoyable. Or, put another way, manners are like fuel—you can own a car without it, but you're not going to get very far.

how to use this book

Each of the following chapters will introduce you to new manners. Some of the topics covered in this book will be familiar to you, while others may be brand-new. We encourage you to read each chapter not only so you can improve your manners but also so you can start thinking of ways you can use these lessons to make others feel comfortable and valued.

Manners are actually a form of loving others. We can show others we love them by showing them respect. By treating others courteously, we are treating them the way we would want to be treated. This is love.

"Do to others as you would have them do to you."
Luke 6:31

"Love each other as I have loved you."
John 15:12

manners matter manners matter manners matter manne

EFFECTIVE introductions

Introductions are important
because we want to make good
first impressions. We all want
to make friends and be liked;
we want to be remembered.

how would you rather be remembered?

- Awkward OR confident?

- Shy OR outgoing?

- Boring OR interesting?

- Lonely OR friendly?

- Dull OR fun?

- Nervous OR relaxed?

- Offensive OR nice?

why else are introductions so important? because people are important.

Every introduction we confront is an opportunity to show others who we really are. Introductions are the first glimpse others see of us—and let's face it, we all want to be remembered as confident, courteous, and considerate. Right?

When you first meet someone, you immediately want to communicate to them that they are important. When you say, "Glad to meet you," you want them to know it's true.

Here are six basic guidelines for introductions; we'll discuss each in greater detail.

Let's take a closer look at these six guidelines.

1. Stand.

2. Smile.

3. Look THE person IN THE eye.

4. Shake HANDS firmly.

5. Listen CAREFULLY.

6. Greet THE person USING their NAME: "Hello, BART. Nice TO meet YOU."

1. Stand.

Even if you are in a seated position when you are introduced to someone, always make the effort to stand. Standing immediately expresses respect and says to the person, "You're important enough to make me get out of my seat." On the other hand, if you simply remain seated when you greet someone, you're communicating the opposite: "You don't mean much to me; you're not worth the energy it takes me to stand up." This may seem like a small matter, but it's not. This is where relationships begin; we want to begin on the right foot.

*Our MANNERS show OTHERS what WE think OF them. THEY also SHOW others WHAT they SHOULD think OF us.

2. Smile.

Believe it or not, most of our communication is done without words. A smile on your face says to others, "It's my privilege to meet you." It's also a way to make others comfortable in your presence. We all know people who rarely smile. Our first impression may be that such people are self-centered, awkward, withdrawn, or perhaps angry. The truth is, they make us feel uncomfortable. We don't want to make others feel this way around us. A genuine smile is the best way to show someone acceptance, favor, and respect.

3. Look THE person IN THE eye.

"The eye is the window into the soul." Eye contact is crucial for an effective introduction. When you look someone in the eye, you're communicating interest, attention, and confidence. On the other hand, if you look away from them, you're expressing disinterest or a lack of focus on the conversation. Failure to look people in the eye can also indicate insecurity or nervousness. If you have trouble maintaining eye contact, be sure to diagnose the cause and work to overcome it.

4. Shake HANDS firmly.

Every culture has a physical expression of greeting. Each is a form of respect and friendship. Some people bow; others kiss on each cheek; some people even rub elbows! In our culture it is acceptable to shake hands. It is our way of acknowledging others and breaking down initial social barriers.

When it comes to shaking hands, there are two extremes:

- Some SHAKE HANDS WITH THE limpness OF A DEAD FISH—gross!
- Others SHAKE HANDS WITH THE gusto OF A NUT CRACKER—ouch!

Try to avoid either extreme. Make your handshake friendly but firm.

5. **Listen** CAREFULLY.
Specifically listen for the person's name and work to remember it. If you don't hear the name clearly, ask for it to be repeated. Don't ever be embarrassed to ask for clarification. It shows that you have respect for the person and that you want to remember their name.

6. **Greet** THE **person** USING **their** NAME.
(This is why we must *listen carefully*!)

"Good morning, Mrs. Lightfoot. It's nice to see you."

such a *greeting* should be loud and clear, just as solid as your handshake.

Using someone's name when you greet them immediately puts them at ease and lets them know you value them. Learning and using a person's name is another way of saying, "You are a significant person to me."

when you can't remember a name

HELLO! My Name is:

No matter how hard you try, you might find that you simply can't remember someone's name. In such a case, you might feel like hiding from that person or ignoring them, but there's a better way.

• you can use the direct approach:

"Hi, my name is Andrea Smith. What's your name?" While this approach will most likely deliver us the goal of learning the person's name, it leaves out the admission that we have met them before but have forgotten their name.

• we recommend the honest approach:

"Hi, I know we've met before, but I'm sorry, I've forgotten your name. I'm Andrea Smith."

This is a much better way to put yourself and the other person at ease. Chances are you will have saved them the embarrassment of asking for your name again, too!
If there happens to be an instance when you know a person but you're not sure they remember you, be thoughtful and proactive.

"Hello, Mr. Buckthorn. My name is Andrea Smith."

introductions in
other cultures

If you are meeting a visitor from another country and you are in America, it is appropriate to greet them as you would anyone else—with a handshake. However, keep in mind that they may not be accustomed to greeting this way. Here is an example of how to greet someone from another culture who is not living in America:

"Hello. My name is Joanna. In my country we greet by shaking hands. Do people in your country use a different greeting?" (If they do use a different greeting, try it out! This is a great way to make the person feel at ease.) There may be a time when you are overseas, perhaps on a mission trip, and you are introduced to someone of another culture. Do a little research before your trip. It's always wise to learn the proper actions or greetings in that particular part of the world before you arrive. If you are unsure, it's safe to follow the lead of the person whom you are meeting. If they offer to shake your hand, extend yours. If you are still in doubt, it is always safe to smile.

Unfortunately, Americans often have the reputation of being loud and obnoxious. What is acceptable behavior in our country may not be tolerable in another. Keep in mind that you are a guest in that country and you should always abide by the social norms of that culture. Cultural sensitivity is always the best approach.

when you are being
introduced

- Listen carefully. Focus on the name of the person you are being introduced to; if you don't hear it clearly, politely ask for the name to be repeated.

- Be courteous. Smile and say, "It's very nice to meet you, Sarah."

- Listen for conversation cues. If your friend introduces you to someone who plays on his flag football team, and you're a big fan of that sport yourself, this opens up an opportunity for conversation.

- Wait until the introductions are complete before conversing with others.

- If someone you've recently met mispronounces your name, politely correct the mistake as soon and as graciously as possible. Ignoring it will only cause more embarrassment down the road.

how to introduce others

Now that we're comfortable meeting new people, let's learn how to introduce people to others.

- Be sure the people you are introducing are paying attention to you.

- Introduce people by the names and titles they prefer.

- Pronounce both names loud and clear.

- Try to put everyone at ease. It helps to mention something about them in addition to their name.

  "Mr. Goodnews is my Bible teacher at school."

- When introducing an older person, use their name first.

  "Grandma, this is my boyfriend, Josh Spurgeon. Josh, this is my grandma, Mrs. Hartley."

- When you are in a large group, only introduce your friend by name rather than everyone in the group.

  "Hey, everyone, this is Napoleon Thomas. Would you please introduce yourselves to him?"

- In a small group, introduce everyone by name.

"Hey, everyone, this is Napoleon Thomas. Napoleon, this is Pedro, Peter, Pam, and Earl."

when speaking to adults

When addressing adults, it's proper to use their titles followed by their surname (last name). Use "Mr." for all men; "Mrs." for married women; and "Ms." for unmarried women, women whose marital status is unknown, and married women using their maiden name. Widows usually continue to use "Mrs.," and divorcées may use either "Ms." or "Mrs." Unless an adult has given you permission to call them by their first name, never use only their first name when addressing them or when introducing someone to them. Even when you become a legal adult at age eighteen, it is always respectful to honor the elder generation in this way.

If you are addressing an adult and are unsure of their last name, it's appropriate to use the titles "ma'am" and "sir." Some think these words are outdated; however, their use is still proper today.

For example:

"ASHLEY, THIS IS MY FATHER."
ASHLEY WOULD REPLY,
"HELLO, MR. CHERRY. IT'S NICE TO FINALLY MEET YOU."

For example:

"GRANDPA, I WOULD LIKE YOU TO MEET MY FRIEND AL FARLEY."
AL WOULD REPLY, "IT'S VERY NICE TO MEET YOU, SIR."
YOUR FRIEND'S MOTHER ASKS YOU IF YOU WOULD LIKE TO EAT PIZZA.
YOU WOULD REPLY, "YES, MA'AM; PIZZA IS ONE OF MY FAVORITES!"
(If, of course, you know her name is Mrs. Crabapple,
you could reply, "Yes, Mrs. Crabapple.")

These rules apply WHEN YOU ARE ADDRESSING

- a teacher;
- a friend's parent; or
- any adult.

introduction insecurities

"When I meet **new students, I never know** what
to **talk about** with them. **I hate it.** I feel
so **awkward** and **out of place.**"

Don't feel awkward. Remember that manners are meant
to help you avoid embarrassment and put others at ease.
Don't get discouraged. As with most things, it takes a little
practice to become good at making conversation.

"I **can** handle **introductions.** It's **after** I meet a person that I **struggle** with what to talk about **next.**"

In the next chapter we'll learn how to develop meaningful
conversations with people we are getting to know. Here's
a short list of several good questions that can jump-start
good communication after an introduction:

- "Where do you go to school?"

- "Do you play any sports? Instruments?"

- "What music do you like to listen to?"

- "What do you enjoy doing in your free time?"

- "Tell me about your family."

After you ask a question, listen to the response. It's easy to come up with more questions once you hear the answers they give. Before long, you will discover points of common interest that can make for further discussion.

summary

Remember THE basics:
- Stand.
- Smile.
- Look THE PERSON IN THE eye.
- Shake HANDS firmly.
- Listen CAREFULLY.
- GREET THE person USING their NAME.

Stay away FROM rude mistakes:
- Don't look away when speaking with someone. It's easy to get distracted when you're in a crowded room, but failing to maintain eye contact is rude to the person with whom you're talking.

- Don't ask questions that are too personal or bring up subjects that may be private or sensitive to others.

- Never interrupt a person who is speaking to you.

ARE YOU UP for a challenge?

Try this: Go to school or church tomorrow and begin putting these steps into practice with your friends, teachers, and other adults.

Learning how to handle introductions effectively is exciting! You have a whole life full of meeting new people ahead of you. No matter what personality traits you have that may keep you from feeling excited about this, you can still be confident and make others feel at ease around you. Now that you know the basics, you can look forward to opportunities to meet new people. And the more you use these skills, the easier and more natural they will become.

MEANINGFUL **conversation**

Now that we've learned how to make effective introductions, we need to know how to carry on meaningful conversations. Good conversation requires that we show genuine interest in another person and clearly communicate our own thoughts and feelings.

Most of us learned how to talk when we were one or two years old, but we learn how to truly communicate when we are teenagers. None of us were born with the ability to converse with others. It's a skill that must be learned.

Anyone can talk, but not everyone can communicate. We all want to be able to offer intelligent conversation, don't we? Let's learn how!

Asking Questions and Listening

An important part of mastering the art of meaningful conversation is learning how to ask appropriate questions. Equally important is the skill of listening carefully to the answers.

Surface QUESTIONS: These are straightforward questions that have easy answers. They help us learn the facts about someone.

- school, grade, activities

- hobbies, interests, music preferences

- family, siblings, pets

- weather, work, news

Secondary QUESTIONS: These questions help us understand a person's thoughts or feelings.
- "What did you think about the play at school today?"

- "How did you feel when the coach treated you that way?"

- "Why does your family have so many traditions?"

Meaningful QUESTIONS: These questions allow you to dig beneath the surface of someone's life and really get to understand them.

- **Life goals**

  "What do you want to do after you graduate? College? Career?"

- **Thoughts**

  "Who has had the biggest impact on your life?"

- **Purpose**

  "What is the most important thing in your life?"

  "Is there anything in your life that you'd be willing to die for? What?"

- **Faith**

  "Do you know for certain that when you die you will go to heaven?"

  "Suppose for some unforeseen reason you were to die and stand before God, and He were to ask you, 'Why should I let you into heaven?' How would you answer Him?"

When you're first getting to know someone, you want to ask surface questions. Once you're comfortable with that person, you'll naturally move toward asking secondary questions, which will lead to more meaningful questions. Obviously, deep conversation takes time to develop. You wouldn't want to introduce yourself to someone and then immediately ask them to state their life purpose. As your friendship grows, so will the depth of your conversation.

Asking a good question is like playing catch with a baseball. The game is fun only when both players participate. If one person catches the ball but never throws it back, the game will soon end. In the same way, when we are asked a question, we need to respond with more than a simple yes or no. We should respond thoughtfully and in some detail to stimulate deeper interaction with the other person.

"DO YOU HAVE ANY BROTHERS OR SISTERS?"

"YES, I HAVE ONE BROTHER WHO IS A FRESHMAN AT GEORGIA TECH."

"REALLY? MY SISTER GRADUATED FROM GEORGIA TECH AND WE GO TO ALL THE GAMES."

"WOW! SO DOES OUR FAMILY! ARE YOU GOING TO THE GAME THIS WEEKEND?"

"I THINK SO. I'LL CALL YOU AND MAYBE WE CAN SIT TOGETHER!"

"THAT'D BE GREAT!"

Family mealtimes are great opportunities to discuss significant subjects.

Try these conversation starters:

- "What did you learn today that you never knew before?"

- "Did anyone meet a new person today?"

- "Hey, Dad, what do you think about. . . ?"

- "What was the highlight of everybody's day?"

Parents love to express their opinions. They also like feedback. Be sure to share your feelings or impressions with them.

- "Dad, do you like your job? Why? What's the most challenging part of it?"

- "Mom, what do you admire about Dad?"

- "Dad, what do you admire about Mom?"

- "What is everyone looking forward to about tomorrow?"

*What DOES this HAVE TO DO WITH manners?

MEANINGFUL conversation IS AN essential
component OF good MANNERS

because

IT EXPRESSES genuine CARE. IT SAYS, "I care ABOUT
WHAT'S happening IN YOUR life, AND I value YOUR
thoughts AND opinions." MAKING good conversation
IS A skill WE all NEED TO work AT developing.

conversation guidelines

- Respect personal space when you talk with others. Standing too close to the person you're speaking with, even if you're giving them a compliment, could come across as an insult. Unless you are in a very noisy room, you should stay a comfortable 18 inches (or so) apart.

- Body language is important in conversation. Your posture, facial expressions, and eye contact all play a part in communicating to someone how you feel about them and about yourself.

- Go easy on the hand gestures. Using your hands to express a point once in a while is fine.

- Avoid overusing or filling your speech with words such as "like," "um," "whatever," and "you know."

- Talk slowly and clearly.

- Don't talk only about yourself.

- Know when to stop talking and start listening.

good listening

Communication involves give-and-take. Talking is only half the process; there can be no meaningful exchange without listening.

Here is some helpful advice for when you find yourself in a conversation:

- Look the person in the eye to show them you are attentive. Don't get distracted by other people or things around you.

- Smile to express interest (unless the topic dictates otherwise).

- Use interjections (once in a while) to spur the conversation: "Wow!" "Oh no!" "Really?"

- Nod your head to indicate that you understand what the other person is saying.

- Don't interrupt or try to finish someone's thoughts. If you must interrupt, apologize and then ask them to continue.

- Don't yawn or fall asleep.

- Don't look at your watch or look across the room.

- Don't fidget or move around.

off-limit conversation

Meaningful conversation leaves people feeling good about themselves. Unfortunately, some conversations can hurt others. We should never participate in conversations that contain the following:

- private or confidential information

- "dirty" or inappropriate (impolite) jokes

- ethnic jokes

- gossip: saying something about someone behind their back that we wouldn't say to their face

- flattery: saying something about someone to their face that we wouldn't say behind their back

If a conversation that was once fun and harmless suddenly becomes insensitive and hurtful, don't hesitate to say, "I don't want to talk about that any longer," or "I would much rather talk about something else." At times you might just need to walk away.

Without wood a fire goes out;
without gossip a quarrel dies down.
PROVERBS 26:20

inappropriate topics
of conversation

Certain topics are inappropriate to discuss with others. If we bring up these topics, we'll make others uncomfortable. Before we know it, we'll begin feeling embarrassed ourselves. For our benefit and theirs, we should stay away from these topics of conversation.

Topics considered taboo:

- *Money:* It's simply none of our business.
  "How much did your house cost?"
  "How much does your dad earn every year?"
  "How much did you spend to take that vacation?"

- *Sex:* Unfortunately, this has become a commonly misused word and the subject of many conversations today among students. God created sex exclusively for men and women who are married to each other—no one else. Period. Therefore, questions, jokes, or conversations about our private sexuality or anyone else's are always off-limits.

- *Physical flaws:* Teasing is a destructive form of humor. We do it because we want to be funny. We do it because we want to elevate ourselves at others' expense. The main reason some people tease is because they are insecure about themselves. Think about it: If you're confident and self-assured, you have no reason to humiliate someone else. A student who is overweight, has acne problems, or has some physical defect is already painfully aware of it and doesn't need reminding.

self-centered speech

When we're excited about something, we want to share it with others. When we excel in a certain area, we naturally feel good about it. It's normal to want to share our excitement with others, but when our pleasure turns into boasting, we've crossed the line between good and bad manners.

When we begin to brag about ourselves, we become like the "resounding gong" or "clanging cymbal" described in the Bible. In other words, our speech becomes very unpleasant to listen to. Manners, like love, do not boast and are not proud (1 Corinthians 13:1,4).

Remember the purpose of manners—to make others feel how important they are to us. When we speak, we should seek to elevate others more than we elevate ourselves. If you commit yourself to doing this, you'll be surprised how people will be drawn to your friendship.

Let another praise you, and not your own mouth;
someone else, and not your own lips.
Proverbs 27:2

sincere compliments

Let your conversation be always full of grace, seasoned
with salt, so that you may know how to answer everyone.
Colossians 4:6

A **thoughtful, sincere** compliment is like a good back rub—when it touches the right spots with the right force, there's nothing like it! It **relaxes** us and makes us **feel** like we can take on the world.

The **best way** to try out **compliments** is to begin with those **closest** to you—your own family. Start with your **parents.** Do you take time to acknowledge all they do for **you**?

- "Thanks for dinner, Mom, especially for the Tater Tots!"

- "Dad, you're handsome; no wonder Mom married you!"

- "Dad, you really do a great job providing for us. These new track shoes are awesome!"

- "Mom, I noticed you cleaned the bathroom today. Thanks!"

- "Mom and Dad, you always make Christmas so special."

For a real surprise, you can even try out some compliments on your brother or sister. Honest, it won't hurt.

- "My sweater looks great on you!"

- "Wow! You're a really good tennis player. Would you let me beat you sometime?"

- "Your new girlfriend is really good-looking. What does she see in you? . . . Just joking."

- "Even if you weren't my brother, I would still want to be your friend."

- "Maybe we don't always get along, but I still love you!"

for friends

- "You're really fun to be with. You bring out the best in me."

- "I really admire the way you. . ."

- "Everybody needs a friend like you."

for teachers

- "I appreciate all the work you put into teaching this class."

- "You really challenge me to think for myself."

- "I always look forward to coming to this class."

- "Math has never been my favorite subject, but you make it interesting."

*Remember:

WHEN YOU give A COMPLIMENT, YOU must BE sincere. IF YOU really DON'T LIKE YOUR teacher, DON'T pretend IT'S YOUR favorite CLASS JUST TO gain FAVOR WITH HIM OR HER. However, DO START LOOKING FOR positive ASPECTS OF THE CLASS. YOU'LL BE surprised HOW YOUR OUTLOOK WILL improve.

summary

Meaningful conversations take a relationship beneath the surface to develop a significant friendship. Healthy communication involves both speaking honestly and listening attentively.

- Be an attentive listener. Maintain eye contact.

- Practice asking interesting and provoking questions.

- Respond with more information than a simple yes or no.

- Convince others that you are sincerely interested in their lives.

ARE YOU UP for a challenge?

The skill of engaging in meaningful conversation is one that will help you through life no matter what career you choose. The sooner you develop this skill, the more successful you will become at it.

Pick three people in your life right now with whom you want to develop meaningful **conversation**. Write down their names and determine to begin now!

1:                  2:   3:

Chapter 3

TELEPHONE manners

For many of us (especially girls), a great deal of our conversation takes place over the telephone. Cell phones, portable phones, phones that plug into the wall—you name it, we log many hours using them. But just because we use them so often doesn't mean we know how to use them properly. Using the phone without proper manners can cause many bad habits to develop. Because we can't see the person with whom we're speaking, we want to be sure to communicate clearly with our words and tone of voice.

Let's start at the beginning.

When the Phone Rings

1. Use the **proper** greeting:

- "Hello."

- "Good morning."

- "Good evening."

2. Speak clearly and confidently. Remember, your face cannot be seen over the phone. Your voice must "smile" for you. Your tone of voice often says more than your words.

3. If the call is for someone else, say, "Just a moment, please. May I ask who's calling?" Then call the person to the phone—but don't shout! If the person is not in the room, leave the room to get them.

4. If the call is for someone not at home, ask if the caller would like to leave a message or have their call returned. If there is a message, be sure to write it down immediately and make certain that it is delivered.

5. If you're at home alone and you don't know the person calling, it's wise to give limited information. Follow the steps given in point 4 (above). Use the words "we" or "us" instead of "I" or "me" since those words are less likely to signal that you are alone.

Talking to Friends and Relatives

When you answer the phone and discover the caller is someone you know—especially a relative or grandparent—you should acknowledge them. Rather than immediately passing the phone to your parents, take the opportunity to tell them about some of the events in your life and also find out about the events in their lives.

You can tell them about all kinds of things:

- your classes at school

- a project you are working on

- an athletic event

- your friends

- a book you are reading

- new things you are learning

You can ask them about. . .

- how they are feeling

- what they've been doing

- when you'll see them next

This friendly communication shows honor and respect to those in our lives whom we care about. They deserve to hear from us!

This principle applies even to your science teacher at school when he calls to speak to your father:

"**Hello,**" you answer.
"**Hi. This is Mr. Sabertooth. May I speak to Mr. Lawrence?**" (As soon as he said "hi," you recognized his voice.)
"**Oh, hello, Mr. Sabertooth. This is David. How are you this evening?**"..."**Are you watching the big game on TV?**" (He probably hasn't watched a game of football in his life, but you're just being polite and trying to make sure he's still human.)
"**No, I'm just making friendly phone calls to parents tonight.**"
"**Wow. You really work hard. I appreciate that, Mr. Sabertooth. Let me get my father.**"
"**It was nice to speak to you, David. I'll see you tomorrow in class.**"
"**Looking forward to it.**"

Speaking in a friendly and open manner with the right mix of confidence and sincerity goes a long way with people. It may even get you a better grade in science! Well, no one can promise you that, but will you settle for a friendlier Mr. Sabertooth?

When Making a Phone Call

When you make a phone call, you need to realize that in a sense you are entering someone else's home. You are interrupting their space and using their time, and you need to be very polite and respectful.

1. **Before** making the call, **remember** the name of the person you are calling, and also **remember** their parents' names in case an **adult** answers the phone.

2. Always **identify** yourself when you make a call.

3. **Ask** if it's a **good** time to talk.

4. When a **young** person answers, greet them properly: "Hello, this is Robert. May I please speak with Elvis?"

5. When an **adult female** voice answers, say, "Hello. This is Robert. Is this Mrs. Presley?". . ."Yes, Mrs. Presley, it's nice to speak with you, too. May I please speak with Elvis?"

6. If an **adult male** voice answers, say, "Hello, Mr. Presley, this is Robert. How are you today?". . . "May I please speak with Elvis?"

Dialing a Wrong Number

Chances are you'll know the minute someone answers if you have dialed a wrong number. *Don't just hang up.* This can be disturbing (not to mention creepy) to the person who answers.

- Apologize and take responsibility: "I'm sorry; I must have dialed this number by mistake."

- If you call that wrong number *again*, clarify the number you are trying to dial. "I'm so sorry. I'm trying to reach 555-7755." If you have the wrong number, look for the correct number in the phone book or call Information.

Answering Machines and Voice Mail

Even when we're talking to a machine, our manners should begin at the sound of the beep.

- **Talk clearly.** Answering machines can muffle the sound of your voice.

- **Talk slower** than usual. It's likely someone will be writing down the information you give.

- Give your **name** and the **time** of your call.

- **Identify** the person you are calling.

- **Leave** your phone number.

- **Politely** request a return phone call at their convenience.

- Keep it **brief.**

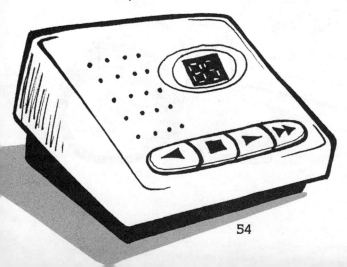

General Telephone Guidelines

- Don't talk to other people around you while you are on the phone with someone. If you must do so, say, "Please excuse me, Stephen. I need to ask my dad a question before he walks out the door." When you return to the conversation, say, "Sorry about that. I'm back."

- Don't eat, drink, chew gum loudly, or blow your nose while you are on the phone. If you find yourself needing to cough, sneeze, or make some other bodily noise that cannot wait, turn the phone away from you and be sure to say, "Excuse me."

- Don't type, wash dishes, vacuum, or do any other noisy activity while on the telephone. All of these can be heard by the other person, and they all communicate disinterest. We might as well tell that person, "You don't have my undivided attention; I have more important things to do than listen to you."

- If someone happens to call when you are in the middle of something important, you may let them know and ask permission to return the call. "Hey, Sandy, I'm sorry, but I told my mother I would finish the dishes. May I call you back in ten minutes?"

- Don't stay on the phone too long. Be respectful of others who need to use the phone.

Cell Phones

Finding a student who doesn't own a cell phone is difficult these days. If you have a cell phone, **pay close attention to these guidelines**. The same general telephone guidelines (see above) apply to cell phone use. Some other rules apply, as well.

- Always turn your cell phone off when you are in a quiet place or an important meeting: church, work, a play, a movie, etc. At the very least, make sure it is silenced. Even the vibrate setting is audible in most cases.

- If, by some horrible accident, your cell phone rings when you are at a formal gathering, *never* answer it. Turn the phone off as soon as you can. Whatever you do, don't let it continue ringing and pretend that it's not your phone!

- *Never* talk on the phone when you are speaking to someone else. This includes everyday instances such as checking out at the grocery store. You should never be talking on your cell phone when you step up to the register. It is unfair to the person you are speaking to on the phone, and it is rude to the person at the register who would like to have your attention and may even want to have a small conversation with you.

- *Never* answer the phone when you are in conversation with someone else. If the phone rings and you are expecting an important call, you may say, "Excuse me. I need to answer this." Most of the calls we receive are not critical, and the best choice we can make is to finish our conversation with the person who is in our presence and return the call when we are free.

- Don't speak loudly when you are using a cell phone. For some reason, many of us think we have to yell, but those cell phone towers are pretty capable! If you must make a call in public, speak as quietly as possible.

- Don't overuse your cell phone. Especially when you're in a public place, don't use your cell phone simply to pass the time.

- Make calls when it is necessary, convenient, and respectful toward others (including your mother and father who are most likely footing your bill).

- Be safe. Using your cell phone while driving makes you four times more likely to be involved in an accident. Already there are some states where it is illegal to use cell phones while driving. If you must use the phone in the car, try using the speakerphone or headset.

Call-Waiting

As a general rule, it is impolite to switch to another line when you are in the middle of a conversation with someone.

- When you are speaking to an adult—especially a family member—you should never answer a call-waiting signal.

  ### Exceptions to this rule:
  - YOUR FATHER OR ANOTHER FAMILY MEMBER IS CALLING AND YOU NEED TO SPEAK TO THEM.
  - SOMEONE IS CALLING FROM ANOTHER COUNTRY.
  - YOU ARE RECEIVING A LONG-AWAITED, VERY IMPORTANT CALL.

- When you are speaking to a friend or someone your age and the caller ID shows that an adult or someone important is calling, it is acceptable to switch to the other line to answer. Make sure to excuse yourself from the conversation first, or tell your friend that you will call her back.

This is an area that requires you to use your judgment; however, it's best to use the call-waiting option sparingly.

Caller ID

Caller ID allows you to see who is calling before you answer the phone. While this option can help your family avoid those annoying sales calls during dinner, it can also get you into some trouble.

- Never answer the phone by saying the person's name, even if you know who is calling: "Hello, Pam." This can be a little creepy. Also, if the caller is actually Pam's older brother, you could suffer some embarrassment.

- Don't avoid answering the phone simply because you have caller ID. Chances are your friends know when you are home and may think you are intentionally avoiding the call. This could cause friction in your relationships.

- If it's not convenient to take a call at that time, that's fine; just be sure to return the call later.

Summary

• Recognize that the telephone should be used with respect.

• Each time you dial the phone, do so with care and courtesy.

• When answering the phone, remember that you represent your family. Be polite, communicating that you're glad the person called. You want others to think highly of your family.

• Speak clearly and confidently.

• Have a smile in your voice.

• Use proper names.

• Use courtesy words such as "please" and "thank you."

• Be sure to end the conversation in a timely manner. You'll probably see the person again soon, and when you do, you want to be sure you still have things to talk about!

ARE YOU UP for a challenge?

God gives us opportunities every day to offer encouragement to people—people like the grocery store attendant or the fast-food worker. Are we too busy to offer them our full attention? Do we make any effort to show them the love of God by offering a kind word? Or are we too busy (on our cell phones) to notice them?

Take this challenge: Use conversation—and the telephone—today to make someone feel valued and special.

PERSONAL manners

Not only are manners guidelines for how to treat *others*; they also teach us how to care for *ourselves*. Often our "unspoken" manners speak louder than what we choose to say or do.

Whether we like it or not, how we look is the quickest introduction to who we are. We've all heard the saying "You never have a second chance to make a first impression." That may seem scary, but it's very true. Sure, once we get to know people better, they may forget the first impression they had of us, but the majority of people we meet will know us only on a very superficial level.

Although it's unhealthy to live your life trying to please everyone around you, you need to realize the importance of showing respect and consideration for yourself and others by the way you dress and groom yourself. Whether you realize it or not, your appearance has a huge effect on the way you are treated and respected.

Each one of us is unique. We were handcrafted by our Creator. The way we treat ourselves is a reflection of the extent to which we value our uniqueness and appreciate God's handiwork.

For you created my inmost being;
you knit me together in my mother's womb.
I praise you because I am fearfully and won-
derfully made; your works are wonderful,
I know that full well.
Psalm 139:13–14

Personal Hygiene

Nothing is worse than discovering too late that we have a problem with our personal manners. None of us want to be teased for the way we look (or smell). We don't want to be ridiculed because of our *hygiene*.

WHAT IS hygiene?

- a system of principles that preserves health

- the application of such principles to our daily lives

More than how we *look*, hygiene is about how we *feel*. Good personal manners allow us to feel good so that we can live life fully and confidently.

We all want to look and feel our best. We want to appear confident and show others that we value the unique way that God made each of us.

It is important to keep in mind that there is a balance when it comes to personal hygiene:

- We should not overdo it by spending too much time on ourselves.

- We should not neglect caring for ourselves and our personal health.

Good Grooming

1. Hair

Hair comes in all colors, textures, and styles. While these characteristics are God-given, the style and grooming of our hair are our responsibility. The way we style our hair is a matter of personal preference. There are, however, certain guidelines that we should follow to care for our hair properly.

- Wash your hair at least every other day, depending on your level of activity and the amount of oil your scalp produces. Greasy is never in style!

- Choose a shampoo that is formulated for your hair type (fine, curly, frizzy, permed, or color-treated). This will make your hair easier to style.

- If you have skin problems such as dandruff, buy a good shampoo that will help.

- Have your hair trimmed regularly and keep it neatly styled. Use products that help keep your hair in place if you need to, but don't overdo it!

67

- Generally, stay away from extreme hairstyles. These detract from the real you and can alienate others whether you intend to or not.

FOR GUYS:

- While it may be popular to grow out your hair and "style" it in a way that looks like you couldn't care less, always be aware that you are making a statement about yourself. If your hair is sloppy and out of control, chances are your attitude will follow. Just keep in mind that the same hairstyle that may be appropriate for a night out with friends may not be the best when showing up for a job interview.

- Keep your beard well trimmed and clean. If you can't grow a beard (only peach fuzz), it's probably best to keep yourself clean-shaven. Also, make sure to shave any excess hair off the back of your neck between haircuts.

2. Body Care

Skin care is not just for women. Healthy-looking skin is an asset for everyone.

- Make it a habit to shower daily even if you choose not to wash your hair each time.

- Choose a soap that is appropriate for your skin type (oily, normal, or dry).

- Apply deodorant/antiperspirant every day. Be careful not to get it on your clothes!

- Be subtle with scents. Apply perfume, cologne, or aftershave sparingly. Don't overpower people by putting on too much. Remember that you want to smell nice, not send people away.

3. Facial Care

- Get in the habit of washing your face at least twice a day—morning and night. If you exercise during the day, it's good to wash your face after you're done.

- Using a moisturizer is helpful. If you have problems with excess oil, use an oil-free kind.

- If you have a problem with acne, ask your parents about consulting a dermatologist who can recommend medication or other lifestyle changes.

FOR GIRLS:

- The best rule for applying makeup is this: *Use sparingly. Less is more.* Makeup should enhance your God-given features and give you a finished look. Heavy makeup should be avoided. A clean and natural look is always most attractive.

- Makeup choices should also be made based on the circumstance and the occasion. (Bright eye shadow would be more appropriate at a concert than at a funeral.)

- Remember: You should always apply makeup in private—not at the dinner table.

4. Tooth Care

It's not your dentist's job to keep your teeth looking nice. Proper dental care is your responsibility.

- Brush with a good toothbrush and effective toothpaste. You should brush at least twice a day—first thing in the morning and last thing in the evening. Ideally, you should brush after every meal to remove food particles from your teeth immediately.

- Flossing is the best way to keep cavities from forming in your teeth and is the most effective way of removing food particles and bacteria from between your teeth. Floss reaches what a toothbrush cannot. Flossing every night before brushing is a good habit to form.

- If it's not possible to brush after you eat, use a breath mint or sugar-free mint chewing gum to remove bad breath.

- If you're worried that you may have bad breath, ask someone like a family member who will be honest with you.

- Remember: "Be true to your teeth, or they'll be false to you!"

5. Nail Care

We use our hands for almost everything we do. People notice our hands; therefore, we need to keep them presentable.

- Keep your nails clean. Make sure there is no noticeable dirt under or around your nails—especially after working in the yard or under the hood of a car.

- Guys, you should keep your nails short. Use clippers once a week to clip and clean both fingernails and toenails if necessary. (Unless, of course, you're trying to beat the guy in India who grew his nails 5 feet long! In that case, good luck!)

- Girls, if you decide to grow your nails long, be careful to file them and keep them from getting jagged. If you polish your nails, maintain the color every week and pick colors that aren't too flashy. (Unless you're going out for the evening.)

- Never bite your nails!

Eating and Sleeping for Your Health

The best way you can care for yourself physically is by developing good eating and sleeping habits. We need good, healthy foods to be able to perform and think clearly. We also need proper sleep. Without it, we can become sick and irritable.

Most people require six to eight hours of sleep each night. Healthy, growing teenagers can require up to ten hours of sleep each night! If you're an athlete and perform strenuous exercise daily, you might need an extra hour of sleep per night.

Proper Dress

Yes, you should wear what you like and what is comfortable. However, you should also dress for the occasion. Just because you love wearing flip-flops doesn't mean you should wear them to the opera in Paris. Simply because something may be "in style" doesn't mean it's appropriate for any occasion.

Individuality and personal expression definitely have their place, but the principles of respect and consideration for others, along with a healthy dose of common sense, should underlie all dressing and grooming decisions.

We need to remember that the clothes we choose to wear and the way we groom ourselves reflect on the respect we have for others and the importance we attach to the occasion. The more we value the event—whether we are attending a wedding or a night out with friends—the more thought and time we should give to dressing.

Formal Dress

There are times when you will be expected to dress up. These occasions include attending church services, graduations, weddings, funerals, fancy restaurants, dinner theaters, and so on.

- For guys, formal dress usually requires a shirt (always with a collar), a tie, dress pants, perhaps a sport jacket, dark socks, and leather shoes.

- Girls should wear a skirt and a nice top (or a dress) and dress shoes. Panty hose are usually preferred, especially in cold weather.

*Some formal events require a tuxedo for men and a formal or full-length gown for women. This kind of attire is usually reserved for prom and other black-tie events.

Casual Dress

We live in a culture that is becoming more casual in the way we are expected to dress. However, *casual* should never be mistaken for *sloppy*.

Certain occasions require "**business attire**" or "**business-casual attire.**"

- For guys, this means a collared shirt and dress pants (khakis or chinos but not denim), dark socks, and leather shoes.

    - For girls, this means a skirt (or dress slacks) and a nice top or a casual dress with tasteful shoes. (Sandals are acceptable for warm weather, but no flip-flops!)

When dressing casually, you may wear just about anything **tasteful**. However, be aware of the activities you may be participating in. You don't want to wear shorts and basketball shoes if your friends are taking you to a nice restaurant or sandals if you'll be mud-wrestling. During summer months, it's acceptable to wear shorts to casual events.

For Girls Only

Girls, when looking for a boyfriend, you are looking for a guy who will **appreciate** you for more than your appearance. You want to be **respected**. The problem is that **many** girls dress as if they don't want a guy to look past their **physical** appearance.

While we all want to show off our personality and our individuality by the way we dress, many girls also want to show off their bodies. Sadly, this doesn't give guys a chance to see who you really are.

Every girl should memorize these two verses from the Bible:

Your beauty should not come from outward adornment, such as braided hair and the wearing of gold jewelry and fine clothes. Instead, it should be that of your inner self, the unfading beauty of a gentle and quiet spirit, which is of great worth in God's sight.
1 PETER 3:3–4

These verses aren't saying that women shouldn't wear braids or jewelry. What they mean is that a woman should **be more concerned with the state of her heart** than with her physical appearance. If her heart is seeking others' attention, she has a problem.

So much more could be said about this subject, but just remember that the **message** we send with our clothes matters more than the clothes themselves.

Here are some questions to ask when choosing what to wear:

- Are these clothes clean? (Good place to start.)

- Do these clothes fit? Too loose? Too tight?

- Who will be there? Would these clothes offend anyone I will be with?

- Will I draw undue attention to myself by wearing this outfit?

- Are these clothes suitable for the type of event/activity/environment I am dressing for?

- Do I feel good about myself and my appearance?

For Guys Only

It has become oh-so-popular to adopt the ruggedly hand-some look of Brad Pitt—sporting five-day-old facial hair, a T-shirt and jeans, and flip-flops. This look is okay at a basketball game, but it's considered inappropriate at a more formal event. When attending a formal dinner such as homecoming or prom, show consideration for your date by shaving and going for a clean look. You can always show your individuality by choosing a special tie or tuxedo vest. (Oh, and please leave the flip-flops in your locker.)

Always remember

to take off your hat to show respect:

at mealtime,

during a public gathering,

while praying,

and when the national anthem is played.

Of course, hats should never be worn

in church,

to an interview,

or at any formal event.

Finding Your Style

Style is an individual thing. It's not about filling your closet with expensive clothes and the latest trends; it's about being comfortable and confident in your clothes. Finding clothes that fit you and flatter your body type will help you feel good about yourself and your style.

- Remember who you are! Girls are not all shaped the same. God made our bodies as different as our personalities. Don't strive to copy someone else's style. Work to create your own sensible, comfortable style.

- Make sure clothes fit you properly by dressing according to your body type. Understand that *well fitted* and *tight* are two different things. The key is to find clothes and sizes that fit and flatter your proportions.

- Find a color palette that suits you.

- Having trouble finding your style? Shop with someone who will give you an honest opinion, such as a sister, a good friend, or a parent.

Summary

Good manners involve good personal hygiene. Caring properly for ourselves isn't selfish; it's smart and sociable. Clean, healthy people feel better about themselves and therefore have more to offer others.

Wear what you like and what makes you feel good and comfortable, but also be aware of others when making your decisions. Work to find the most appropriate clothes for the occasion.

Do you not know that your body is a temple of the Holy Spirit, who is in you, whom you have received from God? You are not your own; you were bought at a price. Therefore honor God with your body.
1 CORINTHIANS 6:19–20

- We owe it to our friends to be presentable.

- We owe it to ourselves to treat our bodies with respect.

- We owe it to the God who designed us to practice good hygiene and to dress in a way that honors Him.

manners matter manners matter

PERSONAL Values

Personal *manners* keep us clean on the *outside*. Personal *values* keep us clean on the *inside*. This is what matters most!

In chapter 4 we discussed the importance of looking and feeling clean in regard to our bodies. This chapter will cover the values that we must embrace to keep our spirits pure and our hearts acceptable before God.

You could be the most popular student in your high school, but without these values, your friendships will not be meaningful, positive, or healthy.

Something of Great Value

Girls with **glamour** impress guys by the way they **look**.
Girls with **values** impress guys by the way they **are**!

Guys with **charm** impress girls by the way they **act**.
Guys with **values** impress girls by the way they **live**!

Values make a big difference in our lives. They are like the dead bolts on our doors—they keep us from being broken into or getting ripped off. There are many personal values.

We'll look closely at just five of these values:

1. The value of **truth**.
2. The value of **family**.
3. The value of **friends**.
4. The value of **sexuality**.
5. The value of **private property**.

1. The Value of Truth

There is no higher value than the truth. All other values come from this one.

- If we're not truthful, we'll never have any true friends because no one will ever truly know us—at least they'll never know who we *really* are.

- We might think that we impress people with our fake self, but they're not really impressed with us; they're impressed with the false image we project.

- Furthermore, if we're not truthful, we'll never grow up. Growing up means taking responsibility for who we really are—not who we pretend to be.

"You shall not give false testimony against your neighbor."
EXODUS 20:16

If you've gotten into the habit of telling lies, now is the time to stop. You are only hurting yourself. By lying, you are keeping yourself from experiencing relationships as they were truly meant to be—open and truthful.

To break this habit, make an agreement with yourself before God right now that from now on you will only tell the truth. If you should ever lie or exaggerate, go immediately to the person, correct the story, and tell them the truth.

2. The Value of Family

It's easy to take our family members for granted, but it's unfortunate we do this to the people we love most. God created family to give us a secure environment where we can blossom and mature. We need to do our part to make sure that happens at home!

Here are some ideas to show your family members how much you value them:

- Make time each day to talk with each member of your family.

- Look for ways to help others beyond your everyday chores.

- Be your family's biggest cheerleader. Be the first to give a compliment.

- Write notes of encouragement and leave them in surprise places.

- Attend siblings' important events (recitals, athletic competitions, award banquets, etc.) even if they have to sit the bench.

- Instead of complaining, offer to help or find a better way to solve the problem.

- Pray for each family member daily.

- Give hugs and kisses frequently.

3. The Value of Friends

A true friend is a real treasure. We're not talking about someone who happens to be your lab partner; we're talking about someone you're really close to.

If you have a good friend, you don't need a mirror. In other words, a real friend is honest and dependable. You can talk about things in complete confidence. You can share your deepest feelings and know your secrets are safe.

On the other hand, sharing something with a lab partner might be like making an announcement over the school's public-address system—pretty soon the entire school will be talking about it.

A true friend, like a mirror, will always tell you the truth rather than what they think you want to hear.

A friend. . .sticks closer than a brother.
PROVERBS 18:24

It's helpful to distinguish different levels of friendship. As your friendships mature, they become more and more meaningful.

Acquaintances: You know their names but very few details about their lives (a lab partner, for instance).

Surface Friends: You attend the same church, play on the same athletic team, or live in the same neighborhood. You share similar interests but not necessarily the same values.

True Friends: You share common interests and have similar values. You actively and creatively help each other reach common goals.

Intimate Friends: You have the same life goals. You are challenging each other with ways to reach and develop your God-given potential.

4. The Value of Sexuality

Our sexuality is a very special gift. It is so special that it demands to be held in high respect and must be protected.

Sex is not a dirty word; it is a holy word and must be treated with utmost reverence. Our culture has become more and more sexually brazen and careless about the subject of sex. As a student in today's society, you are certainly aware of this unfortunate reality. As Christians, we must be careful to guard our speech and even to guard our ears against such immoral conversation. We must show the world what we believe by the way we live. We believe that sex should be honored and initiated the way God intended—only through marriage.

*You should set strong moral standards, refusing to compromise even if it means losing dates.

- Determine now that you will save yourself sexually until you are married.

- Avoid careless talk about sex or jokes about it.

- If you are at a movie theater or a friend's house watching a movie that is immoral, walk out or ask to change the channel.

- Don't defile yourself physically or mentally.

Associate with friends of good quality if you esteem your own reputation.
It is better to be alone than in bad company.
GEORGE WASHINGTON

5. The Value of Private Property

When we uphold the value of private property, we show proper respect for our possessions and the possessions of others.

Why is this value important?

Because everything we have comes from God and ultimately belongs to God! If we're truly thankful for all that we have—even if we don't think we have much or wish we had more—we must take care of everything God has given us.

Here are a few things we can do to be good stewards of God's gifts to us:

- Take care of all our possessions.

    - clothes, shoes, etc.
    - books, CDs, DVDs, MP3 players, computers, etc.
    - car

- ### Respect the value of money.

  - Don't waste money.
  - Don't always buy the most expensive brands. There are plenty of quality clothing stores that will save you money and keep you looking just as good as the expensive brands would.

  - When borrowing from someone, always return the item in good (or better) condition.

  - Remember to return the item promptly. This will increase your chances of borrowing again.

  - Never steal the property of others.

In addition to spending money wisely, we must learn to save and to give to worthy causes.

- Save money for college, a car, or other future expenses.

- Save for Christmas, birthday, and anniversary gifts for your family and friends.

- Give money to your local church or other needs that you see.

manners matter manners matter manners matter manners matter mann

TABLE manners

We all know the cardinal rule of eating: "Chew with your mouth closed." But what else can we do to avoid making others feel uncomfortable?

If you grew up in my (Andrea's) family, mealtime was the favorite time of the day. Breakfast, lunch, or dinner—it didn't matter. If Mom was cooking, we were excited. Of course, there were those few meals on the rotation we weren't so fond of. Mom always did a wonderful job pleasing us all. My brothers and I learned early on that even if we weren't so excited, we would never let it show.

For some families, mealtime is the only time during the day that everyone is present and together. For this reason, it is very important to bring your best manners to the table. The time you spend with your family should be meaningful and fulfilling. Mealtime is no exception.

One of the things you can do to make mealtime more enjoyable—for yourself and for others—is to learn the guidelines for good table manners. Dining etiquette is important because it allows you to enjoy the finer things in life—good company, good conversation, and good food!

Eating Utensils

There was a time (long ago) when people did not use forks and knives—or even plates! However, over the past four hundred years, a basic set of utensils has emerged—along with a complex system for using them.

Forks, knives, and spoons are the basic utensils, and they come in different sizes for different uses.

· Common place setting

This arrangement is used most often. When your mother asks you to "set the table," this is the place setting to follow.

· Formal place setting

At formal events such as banquets or at fancy restaurants, you will see many more utensils at the table than usual.

How do you remember which utensil to use first?

It's easier than you think. Essentially, you work from the outside to the inside—from the utensils farthest from the plate to those closest to it.

Let's practice:

1. As soon as you sit down, place the napkin in your lap.

2. You may notice a longer spoon; this can be used to stir your tea or other beverage after adding sugar or lemon.

3. If you receive hors d'oeuvres, you may notice a small "fish fork" which is used to eat these small appetizers.

4. Your soup spoon is used to drink your soup—quietly!

5. You can use your butter knife and plate for the bread.

6. When your salad is served, you'll use the outside fork to the left of your plate.

7. When dinner is served, you'll use your dinner fork and knife.

8. Finally, after the meal, you'll use either your dessert fork or spoon, depending on what is served.

Handling Utensils

In kindergarten we all learned the proper way to hold a crayon. Similarly, there is a proper way to hold a spoon, fork, and knife. For normal use, the fork or spoon rests on the middle finger of your hand, with your forefinger and thumb gripping the handle (similar to the way you would hold a pencil as you write—only closer to the other end).

When cutting food, we use a different grip. Hold the fork (tines pointed down) in your left hand and spear the food to steady it, pressing the handle down with your index finger. Hold the knife in your right hand (or reversed if you are left-handed) with your index finger pressed just below where the handle meets the blade.

- Make small, short cuts to avoid shaking the entire table.

- Avoid unnecessary sounds, such as clanging silverware against your plate, scraping utensils together, or worse—screeching your knife across the bottom of the plate.

- Cut one or two pieces of meat at a time. Don't dissect your steak or any other piece of meat at the dinner table. Eat each cut piece before cutting more.

- Place the knife on your plate between mouthfuls. Never hold the knife in one hand while feeding yourself with the fork in the other hand.

*Note: In Europe this technique is actually acceptable. If you happen to visit Europe, or you are European, feel free to eat this way.

- When cutting pieces of food, make sure they are small enough to fit comfortably in your mouth—no matter how hungry you are.

Other Guidelines to Remember

The only utensils used to put food in your mouth are the fork and spoon—never the knife. The spoon is used only for eating soups and desserts or for stirring drinks. The spoon should not be used for drinking coffee or for eating the meal.

Once you have started eating, keep your knife and fork on your plate. Don't place them back on the table after using them. Don't lean them in such a way that they are partly on the table and partly on your plate. If your knife or fork accidentally falls off your plate, calmly pick it up and rest it back on your plate (unless it falls on the floor—then you may ask the server for a new one).

When you have finished your meal, place your knife and fork on your plate parallel (side by side) to each other. This will indicate to the server that you have completed your meal.

The Napkin Is Your Friend

The napkin is designed to keep you from public embarrassment and should be kept within reach at all times. It is usually located to the left of your plate. Occasionally you'll find it folded on top of the dinner plate or perhaps even inside the (empty) drinking glass to the right of your plate.

Napkin Do's

• After sitting down, immediately place the napkin in your lap.

• Only use the napkin to blot your mouth or wipe your hands.

• Use only one side of the napkin so that it can lie in your lap without getting you dirty or staining your clothes.

• Leave the napkin lying flat in your lap.

Napkin Don'ts

• Don't leave the napkin on the table.

• Don't use the napkin as a bib by tucking it into your shirt collar or tying it around your neck.

• Don't use the napkin as a handkerchief; never use it to blow your nose.

• Don't use the napkin to wipe your entire face— only your mouth.

The Beverage

Glasses (the kind you drink from) come
in all different sizes. There are essentially
three basic shapes from which we drink.

The normal glass:
Hold a normal glass toward the middle or bottom so your fingers never touch the rim. This
is especially considerate when you are serving your guests.
To avoid spreading germs (and as a basic courtesy), never
touch the glass where they have placed their mouth or will
be placing their mouth.

The goblet:
Hold a goblet by the bottom of the bowl (the round center
of the goblet). Never hold it by the stem or base. Holding
the bowl allows for a better grip.

The mug:
Hold a cup by the handle. If the
cup contains a hot beverage such
as coffee or hot chocolate, it's
almost impossible to hold the
cup itself. The handle is designed
to avoid burning. Use it.

*Eating and drinking should always be done as quietly as possible. No slurping or sloshing—and, of course, no burping.

Sitting
at
the
Table

When eating at home, many of us have the same seat at every meal. When eating at a friend's house, it is polite to wait to be seated until your friend shows you where you should sit. At a formal banquet, place cards will indicate where to sit.

- It is polite to wait to be seated until the host is seated or until he or she asks everyone to sit.

- Men should pull out the chairs for the women next to them, helping them to be seated first.

The Blessing

God created [foods] to be received with thanksgiving. . . .
For everything God created is good, and nothing is to be
rejected if it is received with thanksgiving, because it is
consecrated by the word of God and prayer.
1 TIMOTHY 4:3–5

Before meals is a good time to pause and thank God
for the meal and for His provision. This prayer may
be called *grace*, the *blessing*, or *returning thanks*. It
doesn't have to be long. As the brothers in the Hartley
household used to joke, "This is no time to catch up
on your devotional life." Mealtime prayers should be
simple and brief.

If you're at a friend's home and they don't pause to
say a blessing, as you're comfortable doing, don't
say anything about it. Simply thank God silently
before you begin eating and enjoy the meal. The
host is the one who decides whether or not to say
the blessing.

On the other hand, if you are the host and you
have a friend to your house or to a restaurant,
you should feel free to lead in a short prayer.
Simply say, "I always thank God for my food
before I eat. Let me lead us." Then bow your head
and pray.

When to
Start
Eating

When everyone is seated at the table, it's polite to wait for the host to raise his or her fork from the table. This gesture indicates that the meal may begin.

There may be times when the host has given you permission to begin eating without him or her. In this case, it is acceptable to start the meal.

*If you ever have a doubt about which utensil to use, just watch the host. Use the same utensil they do.

Soup

When eating soup, **keep a few rules in mind**. Before taking a big spoonful of soup from the middle of the bowl, **carefully** check the temperature. If the soup is too hot, gently stir it to allow heat to escape. Skim the top of the bowl with your spoon to get cooler swallows. Never blow soup and never slurp.

When using a larger soup spoon, you should never try to stick the entire spoon in your mouth. Drink soup from the tip or side of the spoon. As you near the end of the bowl, it's okay to tilt the bowl slightly to get the last spoonful. **Never pick up the bowl to drink from it**.

When you're finished, leave the spoon in the bowl or on the plate beneath the cup. Never put the spoon back on the table.

Bread and Butter

Always place bread on the bread and butter plate. When selecting a roll from the basket, never doubt your choice. As soon as you touch it, you can't put it back. Choose wisely.

Use the butter knife *only* to transfer butter to your bread plate; don't use it to butter your bread. Instead, use your dinner knife to butter your bread. Break off a bite-size piece of your bread or roll, butter it, and then eat it. Never butter the entire piece of bread or roll at one time.

Passing Food

- When passing a glass, never touch the rim.

- When passing serving dishes, always be sure to pass the serving spoon or fork along with the dish. Never leave it on your own plate.

- Food is normally passed to your right—counterclockwise—unless your host directs differently.

- Take only as much food as you can eat. When you serve yourself, be sure there is enough food to allow each person at the table a similar-size serving.

- When trying a food for the first time, consider that you may not like it. In this case, it's better to take a small amount. If you do enjoy the taste, you can always ask for more.

- If you take some food that you don't enjoy, just leave it on your plate without commenting on your displeasure. (You may be thinking, *Yuck!* but you shouldn't say it.)

Dessert

For many of us, dessert is our favorite part of the meal. Even though we're looking forward to it, we still want our manners to show.

- Spoons are used for soft desserts—custard, pudding, ice cream, sherbet.

- Forks are used for solid desserts—cakes, cobblers, pies, fruit.

- If nuts or candies are served, take a few and place them on your plate. Eat them from your own plate. Never eat them directly from the serving dish.

Miscellaneous
Table Manners

- If you need something on the table that is not next to you, ask to have it passed to you. Never reach.

- Eat most food with a knife and fork unless the host gives permission otherwise. On a picnic, using your fingers is fine.

- Always taste food before seasoning it. Overseasoning your food may insult not only the person who prepared the meal, but also your taste buds.

- Always chew with your mouth closed and wait to speak until you have swallowed.

- Never take a drink while still chewing food (unless you are choking).

- Don't rest your elbows on the table during the meal. Before or after the meal, this is acceptable.

- Sit up straight while eating. Never lower your head to pick up your food. Always lift the food to your mouth.

• Hold only a single utensil at a time. The exception is when cutting food or pushing small food (such as corn or peas) onto your fork. Otherwise, you should place the knife on your plate while you feed yourself.

• If a certain food doesn't appeal to you, take a small amount. If the thought of it being on your plate makes you sick, graciously pass it by without commenting.

• If you need to use the restroom during the meal, simply ask, "May I please be excused for a moment?" Don't ask, "Can I use your bathroom?"

• Never hand-feed pets from the table during any meal.

Tasteful Conversation

Now is the time to use what we learned in chapter 2 about meaningful conversation. No matter how good the food may be, mealtimes are always more enjoyable with good conversation.

- If there is anyone at the table you don't know, introduce yourself.

- When eating with a group, make an effort to engage in conversation with everyone at the table.

- If anyone at the table is sitting silently, try to make them feel included. Ask creative questions to draw them into discussion.

- Don't dominate the conversation. Only share important details or general observations. No one enjoys a filibuster at mealtime.

- Mealtime conversations should be positive and pleasant, nothing too heavy. Avoid confrontations or arguments. These tend to create loss of appetite. Save these for other environments if they must occur.

- When talking at the table, don't speak with your hands or make big gestures—certainly not while holding utensils.

After the Meal

- Just as you thank God before the meal, remember to thank the host or cook after the meal.

- Never leave your place at the table until the host gives you permission.

- At your own home, always clear your plate and glass. At a friend's home, offer to help clear the table or help with the dishes.

- When you rise from the table, push your chair back under the table. Place your napkin unfolded next to your plate.

What
If?

1. "What if I have something in my mouth that I absolutely cannot swallow? How do I get rid of it?"

> The general answer to the question is this: The means you used to get it into your mouth is the means you should use to get it back out.
>
> - If it is a bad piece of meat, remove it with the fork you are using.
>
> - If it is soup that is burning your mouth, remove it by spoon.
>
> - If it is a watermelon seed from a piece of watermelon that you ate by hand, remove it with your fingers or with a napkin.
>
> Never spit anything directly onto your plate. Always remain calm and try not to draw attention to your predicament.

2. "May I use my roll to soak up gravy or other sauces left on my plate?"

> Yes! Just do it with your fork, using bite-size pieces of bread.

113

3. "May I use a knife as a 'pusher' when eating peas or corn?"

Yes! You may also use your roll as a pusher. Just don't eat with both hands. After you use your fork to eat your corn, put down your fork and then take a bite of roll.

4. "What if I spill?"

It's going to happen to all of us. We all make mistakes when we eat. Obviously, we try to eat as mannerly as possible, but when we spill, we apologize, help clean it up, and enjoy the rest of the meal.

5. "What if I have to burp?"

Belching is never encouraged. If it is absolutely necessary, it should be done quietly and as infrequently as possible. If you must burp, do it once and say, "Excuse me," to no one in particular. If you find this becoming a problem, it would be polite to excuse yourself from the table.

6. "What if I get food caught between my teeth?"

If your tongue is unable to remove the food (with your mouth closed, of course) wait until after the meal and find a toothpick or use dental floss in the privacy of the bathroom. Toothpicks are acceptable only after the meal and away from the dinner table.

7. "What if the person next to me is making me sick because of all the noise he is making eating with his mouth open?"

> Don't correct the person during the meal. This is usually too embarrassing even among friends. However, if you care about the person, do him a favor—tell him his problem after the meal is over and in private. You may even want to give him a copy of this book!

8. "What if I'm at a friend's house and I don't like any of the food served?"

> Take a very small portion of the least repulsive food served. There must be something you can eat without getting sick. Be sure to compliment your host on the effort he or she put forth in preparing the meal, even if you can't sincerely compliment the meal itself.

Summary

Before Meals

- Use the restroom.

- Wash your hands.

- Wait for the host to be seated.

- Place the napkin in your lap.

- Thank God.

- Wait for the host to raise his or her fork.

During Meals

- Chew with your mouth closed.

- Pass food to the right.

- Say "please" and "thank you."

- Practice good posture.

- Enjoy good conversation.

After Meals

- Thank the host or cook for the meal.

- Ask to be excused.

- Clear your plate, utensils, and glass.

- Push your chair under the table.

ARE YOU UP for a challenge?

We covered several guidelines in this chapter concerning table manners. It seems like a lot to remember when you're trying to enjoy your meal. The good news is that you've probably been using some of these strategies already.

Rather than trying to implement all of these guidelines at once, read back through the chapter and select three manners you would like to begin practicing now. Perhaps there are a few manners you know you need to work on immediately. When you feel you've mastered those three, pick three more and begin working on those. Remember, manners are not learned all at once. They take time to master.

When you have decided on the three new manners you would like to implement, write them in the spaces below.

1.

2.

3.

manners matter manners matter manners matter manners

RESTAURANT manners

We all enjoy eating out. We all have our favorite restaurants. Styles range from cafeterias to buffets; from fast-food places to gourmet. Since there are so many restaurants to choose from, it's helpful to understand the different requirements when eating in such places. The way we conduct ourselves when we eat at home or at a friend's home is different from the way we would behave in a restaurant.

Fast Food

By far, the most common and most popular restaurants are fast-food restaurants. The added convenience of not having to get out of your car to eat is something we all love. In our fast-paced society, it's nice to have the option of pulling up to the drive-thru window to order a meal.

Even though these are not fancy places and require only that you wear a shirt and shoes and have a little cash with you, certain manners still apply to this laid-back environment.

When dining inside
fast-food restaurants:

- Be sure everyone at your table has his or her food before you start eating.

- Place food wrappers on the table instead of eating from the bag or tray.

- Be sure to have napkins, straws, and condiments available at your spot.

- Eating with your fingers is acceptable—unless, of course, you ordered a salad or chili.

- Don't be wasteful. If you take 20 ketchup packets and use only 16, be courteous and put the remaining 4 back where you got them. However, keep in mind that at some restaurants employees are required to discard any unused condiment packets and even the unused napkins their customers leave behind, so take only what you truly need.

- Keep your voice at a reasonable level. If you are with a large group, try to find an area in the restaurant where you will not disturb other customers trying to enjoy a nice meal.

- Don't forget to clean up as you leave. If you spilled something on the table, wipe it up. If you spill a drink on the floor, be kind and notify an employee of your accident.

Buffets
and
Cafeterias

The biggest mistake you can make at a cafeteria is filling your plate with food just because you're hungry and everything looks good as you pass by. As you make your selections, try to mix foods and tastes that will complement each other when you finally sit down to eat. For example, the eggs benedict and the manicotti may not taste so good at the same meal. Instead of placing both items on your plate, fill your plate with a variety of breakfast foods (eggs, waffles, sausage); if you're still hungry after eating those foods, go back again for the manicotti and garlic bread.

- In a cafeteria, plates, utensils, and napkins are alongside the trays at the beginning of the serving line.

- At a buffet, your napkin and utensils will be at your table. Your plate will be at the front of the buffet table.

- Don't be wasteful. It's better to get a small portion at first to make sure you like the food. You can always go back to get more of what you like.

- Most cafeterias have people to collect trays. If not, simply place your tray on the nearby tray stand.

- At a buffet, a server will collect your plate(s) when you're through.

Eating at restaurants with so many choices can actually teach us a valuable lesson in life. We learn that we just can't have everything. Some people try to but leave feeling miserable.

Family Restaurants

Family restaurants offer sit-down dinners. This means you don't stand in line for your food as you would for fast food or in a buffet or cafeteria line. The food is prepared and brought to your table. These restaurants are more expensive than fast food but have a much larger selection.

- When you're shown to your table, you'll usually find your silverware wrapped in your napkin. In such a case, it's your job to set the silverware out as you would when eating at home.

- Family restaurants don't always provide butter plates. In this case, put your butter and bread on your dinner plate, never on the bare table.

- When you are finished using sugar packets, cracker wrappers, or butter containers, place the empty material in the ashtray (these are found in fewer places now) or under the edge of your plate.

- You may find that only one fork is provided for your meal. If you order salad, remember to save your fork for the main course when your salad plate is removed.

*Never feel embarrassed to bow your head in a restaurant to thank God for your food.

Servers

Servers are people, too, and they deserve to be treated properly. Try to remember your server's name. If they forget to tell you their name, ask for it before they leave the table. You'll find that calling them by name will make them feel at ease and promote good service.

- When ordering, say, "*May I please have* the grilled cheese platter?"

- When you are served, say, "Thank you." Even if it's something as simple as a drink refill, always acknowledge your server by saying these two words.

- When you have a need, a question, or a problem, discreetly call your waiter. Do this only when he is on his way from table to table—not busy with other customers. This is best done by a hand gesture rather than by voice. Calling aloud may disrupt the entire restaurant. Never get attention by snapping your fingers, clapping your hands, or tapping on a glass. If they are close enough to hear you in normal conversational volume, you may call them by name— *always* with a smile.

Tipping

When you have finished dining at a restaurant where you have been waited on by a server, you should leave a tip, or *gratuity*, of 15, 18, or 20 percent of the cost of the meal. Realize that tips account for much of the server's earnings. If your server does an exceptional job, it's nice to tip more. If the service was poor, you should still leave a tip of 10 to 15 percent, but register a complaint with the manager.

Sometimes, especially for large groups, the gratuity is automatically added to the bill. It's always wise to check your bill to make certain the gratuity hasn't already been added. However, if your server was very helpful and efficient in serving your large group, it would be kind to give her a bonus to say thank you.

*Note: Tipping is also advised when getting your hair cut, when getting your nails done, and of course when having a pizza delivered.

"Fancy"

Gourmet

Restaurants

- Eventually each of us will have an opportunity to eat at a fancy restaurant during one of these occasions:

- your parents' anniversary

- a wedding

- prom or a graduation banquet

- other special occasions

- Make sure to dress for the occasion: tie and jacket for guys and a nice dress for girls. On certain occasions (such as prom and homecoming) it's appropriate for the guy to purchase a corsage for the girl.

- The man who shows up to seat you at the table is the *maître d'*. Since the meal is *gourmet*, it will be more expensive. Therefore, it's thoughtful not to order a meal that's more expensive than the person paying the bill can afford. If you are paying, the choice is yours.

• If you drop silverware, leave it on the floor. It's neither sanitary nor mannerly to pick up dropped utensils. Your waiter will be glad to replace it.

• When squeezing a lemon, cup your hand around it to avoid squirting lemon juice across the room.

• At a formal dinner, whenever a woman rises from the table, all men should stand, as well. The man seated nearest to her should help her move her chair. When she returns, all men should stand once again and reseat themselves only after she is seated.

The Gourmet Menu

There are **two basic types** of food service in a fancy restaurant:

- *table d'hôte:* one price for a complete meal

- *à la carte:* each course priced separately

Be sure to read your menu **carefully** before ordering. If you are uncertain about a particular food or the cost of a certain item, ask questions. A full meal may include an appetizer, soup, salad, main course (entrée), dessert, and beverage. If you know you can't eat that much, ask to skip one or two courses, or order à la carte. Many restaurants include a salad and a vegetable with your entrée. Always ask your server when in doubt.

Many finer restaurants offer a small sorbet (sherbet) after the salad course. This chills the taste buds and clears the taste in your mouth before the main course.

Crackers are served with the soup course. No matter what you do at home, this in not the time to crumble the crackers and drown them in your soup. If you must, place crackers in the soup and crumble them (quietly) using your spoon.

Menus often contain foreign words that you may not understand. If in doubt, ask your server, who will be glad to explain any words or dishes that raise questions.

Foreign Words
on Menus

à la . . . . in the style of
à la king. . . . . in cream sauce
almondine. . . . . with almonds
au jus. . . . . in its own juice
bonbon . . . . candy
consommé . . . . clear soup
crepe (or crêpe). . . . . thin pancake
croutons . . . . diced toasted bread
demitasse. . . . . strong black coffee
en croute . . . . baked in pastry crust
escargot . . . . snails
filet mignon . . . . grilled choice beef
flambé. . . . . served flaming
Florentine . . . . with spinach
frappé . . . . chilled
fruits de mer . . . . seafood
garni. . . . . decorated
gratiné . . . topped with bread crumbs and cheese

130

hors d'oeuvres . . . . .appetizers
julienne . . . . thin strips
lait. . . . . milk
legumes . . . . vegetables
madrilene . . . . .clear chilled soup
maison . . . . house (restaurant)
Mornay . . . . .white cheese sauce
mousse . . . . . . .light dessert of cream and eggs
omelette. . . . . egg dish
parfait. iced dessert
petit . . . . small
poisson. . . . . .fish
purée. . . . . mashed
quiche. . . custard pie with eggs and cheese
sorbet . . . . fruit sherbet
soufflé . . . . puffed dish with eggs and cheese
tart . . . . small fruit pie
vichyssoise . . . . cold potato soup

Do I Eat It with My Fork, Spoon, or Fingers?

When is it okay to use your fingers to eat certain foods? It depends on where you are. For example, if you're at a picnic or a fast-food joint, fingers are acceptable for most things. However, if you're eating in a dining room or gourmet restaurant, you'll want to use your fork or spoon if you can.

Here are some helpful guidelines:

Celery, carrot sticks. . . . . Fingers

Corn on the cob . . . . Fingers

French fries (fast-food place, picnic) . . . . Fingers

French fries (dining room). Fork

Fried chicken (picnic) . . . . Fingers

Fried chicken (dining room) . . . . Fork

Watermelon (picnic). . . . . Fingers

Watermelon (dining room) . . . . Fork

Strawberries or dessert . . . . Fork

Cut fruit on dinner plate . . . . Fork

Dry, crisp bacon . . . . Fingers

Lobster in shell,
     chilled shrimp served as appetizer. . . . . Fingers

RESTAURANT No-no's

Never, never...

- Blow your straw paper across the room. (Remove it with your fingers.)

- Blow bubbles with your straw.

- Talk loudly and boisterously while in a restaurant.

- Play music by rubbing your fingers along the rim of the glass.

- Write on cloth tablecloths. (It's okay to write on paper place mats designed for personal artwork.)

- Build houses out of sugar packets or coasters.

- Pour sugar in the saltshaker.

- Play pranks by unscrewing the lids of salt, pepper, or cheese dispensers.

manners matter manners matter
manners matter manners matter
manners matter manners matter
manners matter manners matter
manners matter manners matter
manners matter manners matter
manners matter manners matter
manners matter manners matter

Chapter 8

PARTY manners

You may not consider yourself a "party animal," but we all get invited to parties—birthday parties, graduation parties, holiday parties—parties for all occasions.

When parties are fun, we don't even notice the manners that govern our celebration. But when party manners are overlooked, the fun disappears faster than the potato chips. The following guidelines are designed to keep us from some of those embarrassing situations.

Invitations

Every party begins with an invitation. Informal parties are announced by telephone. When it's your party and you're doing the inviting, be prepared to give the type of event, date, and time. Also be sure to give directions to your home.

More formal parties are announced by written invitation. These are usually sent out a week or two before the event in order to give people a chance to check their schedules and reserve the date.

Example of a Written Invitation

You Are Invited to a. . .
Birthday Party
for Lily Smith
11:00 a.m.
Saturday, November 11, 2006
2300 Pleasant Place, Town
RSVP (555) 555-5577

RSVP: These are four very important letters.
They are the first letters of four French words that mean **"respond if you please."** In other words, "Call me as soon as possible to tell me if you'll be able to attend."

When we receive invitations with those four letters, we want to give people the courtesy of replying immediately with a yes or no.

Plan Ahead

Before you arrive at a party, know what to expect. If it's a birthday party, be sure you know whether a gift is appropriate or expected. If so, discover what the guest of honor would enjoy.

If you'll be spending the night, be sure to bring all necessary items, including your toothbrush and clean underwear. Always bring a pillow and sleeping bag unless you are told otherwise.

Always be on time!

Always check on the **appropriate** dress code.

- casual

- informal

- semiformal

- formal

- costume

- swimwear

*Be sure you are dressed properly for the occasion.

The Art of Mingling

Some people would much rather stay at home than go to a party. The thought of being around a crowd of people and having to talk to everyone sounds about as much fun as having a root canal. If this is you, take heart! The life of the party probably isn't nearly as funny as he thinks he is. Chances are, no matter what your personality or temperament, another person at the party will feel just like you. Look around, find the nearest introvert (probably someone standing in the corner), and have a creative conversation.

Avoid isolating yourself. Interact even if you don't have a pocketful of one-liners. If someone is alone, introductions are easy. If you're sitting next to a nonstop talker, be a good listener. Good listeners are rare! When joining in on group conversation, just listen for a subject you enjoy or a lull in the conversation and jump right in.

Somebody went to a lot of trouble to throw the party. You accepted the invitation. You might as well have a good time!

Keeping Pure at Parties

Parties can turn out differently than we expect. As a Christian student in today's world—whether you attend a public or Christian school—you will no doubt face many challenges and temptations. **Drugs, alcohol, sex, witchcraft, pornography**—these are just some of the traps that teenagers are lured into by their "friends."

Choosing *not* to attend a party where you know these things will be present is smart. However, sometimes you won't discover what's happening at the party until you get there. That's why it's important to decide these things *now*:

- **Your body belongs to God.**

- **You are not going to harm your body, mind, or spirit—no matter what anyone else says.**

- *Whatever it takes*, **and with God's help, you will keep yourself clean and pure from these harmful traps of the enemy.**

The Lord allows us to face difficult situations and choices to make us more mature in our faith. He also promises that He will never give us more than we can handle, and He promises us a way out of temptation. (1 Corinthians 10:13).

It's Time to Go

- Say a pleasant "Good night" to everyone.

- Thank your friend who hosted the party and the parents (if they are present).

- If you have time, volunteer to help clean up before you leave.

- If anyone has been drinking at the party, don't let them drive home. Find a sober driver or call their parents to pick them up.

- It's always thoughtful to tell your parents a little about the party. They don't need to hear all the details, but they like to know you had a good time.

Summary

- Tell the host of the party if you plan to attend.

- Arrive at the party on time (but not early).

- Be a willing participant in (appropriate) party activities.

- Offer to help when you can.

- Be sure to thank the party host (twice if you can).

- Have fun!

DATING manners

Dating rules have changed over the years. Once upon a time, the guy would do the asking and the paying. He would pick the time and the place. The girl would comply with every detail and look on with wide-eyed admiration of her date's chivalry and graciousness. Dating was also considered to be a serious and necessary step on the road toward marriage, babies, family obligations, and so on.

Dating today is much different. It is casual and much less clear-cut. However, one thing has not changed—the power of manners. Practicing good manners is one of the most effective ways not only to get a date but to ensure that you are relaxed and have fun while dating. . .and to bolster the likelihood of future dates! Sound like a big promise? Read on.

The Invitation—Girls

This may sound old-fashioned, but it is still considered appropriate for the guy to take the initiative of asking a girl on a date. There are exceptions (see below). But no matter what society tells you or what your friends are doing, it's natural for guys to want to be (and they should be) the leader or pursuer in the relationship. Girls, if you're honest with yourselves, you want this, too. You love the feeling of being chosen and pursued. You want someone who will take charge. God created you to be this way!

Here are the exceptions:

- A girl who attends a different school than her boy friend should feel free to invite him to her high school prom.

- Many schools hold Sadie Hawkins dances to which the girls are required to ask the guys.

- A girl may invite a guy to join her for a group date or ask a "friend" to a sporting event she happens to have tickets to.

The main thing to remember, girls, is that you shouldn't be seeking a boyfriend every minute of the day. You'll find that guys are actually attracted to girls who are *not* wrapped up in dating, but rather focus more on others than themselves.

The Invitation—Guys
When asking a girl on a date. . .

- Don't be afraid to ask her in person, face-to-face. This shows confidence. It also gives you a better chance of getting a yes in reply.

- If you do call her on the telephone, make sure to have all the details. (When, where, who else will be there, and when you will be home.)

- If you really want to score some points—especially on a first date—ask to speak to the girl's father to ask permission before speaking to her. This may seem *scary*, but it shows respect not only for her but for her parents.

- Don't wait until the last minute. Allow several days' notice.

- If you're planning a special activity (such as paintball), tell her so she can dress appropriately and plan accordingly.

- Be prepared to pick her up for the date. If you can't drive, make sure you've secured a driver for the event ahead of time.

- If the girl says no, don't argue or question why. Respect her decision and don't take it personally.

The Big Date—Guys

Now that you have a date, your work has only just begun! Relax—this is the fun part!

- Arrive a few minutes early to meet her parents—not too early, or you may spend more time than you'd like looking at her father's gun collection. Remember that girls take all the time they are given to get ready.

- If you're running late, call. Even if you arrive late, you should go inside to meet the parents.

- Go to the door for every date. Never honk the horn and expect her to come out to the car. If it's raining, bring her an umbrella.

- Greet her parents by their last name using "Mr." or "Mrs." Offer a firm handshake and always look them in the eye when speaking. Be prepared to have a short conversation with them while you wait for your date.

- Make sure her parents know where you will be and when you will have her home.

- Always be aware of the time. Aim to have your date home 10 to 15 minutes prior to curfew just to be safe.

Anyone can take a girl on a date, but it takes a gentleman to treat her like a lady.

- Open her car door and any other door you come to.

- Let her walk in front of you through doorways or narrow entryways.

- Assist her with her coat.

- Help carry anything heavy she may have. (Except her purse—that's her problem!)

- Help her get seated at the table.

- Ask her if she is comfortable. Notice if she is cold during dinner or in the car.

- Look for other ways to make her night more enjoyable.

*It's in these little gestures that girls feel special and respected.

The Big Date—Girls

Remember that your date already finds you special; after all, he asked you out. *Be yourself!*

• Be ready for your date on time, especially if your date has arrived and is downstairs talking to your parents for the first time.

• Remember to make sure you are dressed appropriately and modestly. (If in doubt, you can always ask your dad or brother.)

• Always bring money along just in case your date doesn't pay (which may be his last date with you). At any rate, be prepared.

• If your date opens the car door for you, it's always nice to reach over and unlock his door if it's still locked.

• Be active in the conversation. Get to know your date. Instead of talking about yourself, ask questions about him that stimulate conversation.

• Listen! Don't think you have to comment on everything being said.

• Be sure to express your appreciation along the way. When he opens your door, say "thank you." When he pays for your meal, be sure to thank him. A guy always likes to hear that you're enjoying yourself. This puts him at ease.

Be Creative

Dating can be so predictable sometimes. It's easy to get caught in the rut of movie, burgers, mall, another movie, video games, back to the mall, more burgers. . .

Everyone enjoys doing something different:

- Go on a picnic.
- Take a hike on a nature trail.
- Go on a bike ride.
- Visit the park and ride the swings.
- Build a sandcastle.
- Borrow a video camera and make your own movie.
- Go fishing or canoeing.
- Watch a Little League or soccer game.
- Plan a cookout.
- Go horseback riding.
- Take tennis lessons.
- Try miniature golfing.

Doing something creative doesn't cost much more than a movie or a pizza, and some of the ideas listed above are free. Try doing something different, and chances are you'll find out something new about your date.

Your Sexuality

The most obvious means of showing disrespect for your date is to violate them sexually or morally. This is an area you must treat with greatest respect and care. As we discussed in chapter 5, "Personal Values," our bodies and certainly the private parts of our bodies are precisely that—private. They should not be exposed to, touched by, or talked about with other people. It's very important to maintain strict standards so that you don't offend a boyfriend or girlfriend. Most important, we want to remain pure before our Maker and Creator. We're not talking about safe sex; we're talking about *no sex* until marriage.

When you face temptation to do things you know are wrong, there are a number of approaches you might take:

- Don't date alone; stay in groups of friends.

- Avoid drinking or hanging around students who drink.

- Don't allow any opportunity for sexual sin. Stay away from tempting situations.

  - Never be alone with your date at each other's home. Never, not even when babysitting.

    - Stay physically active—playing tennis, running, hiking, biking, skiing, swimming.

    - Dress modestly.

    - Pray before your date. Ask God to protect you against sin and convict your heart when it goes astray.

You can never be too careful in this area of dating. Even though you may think your date is a nice person, don't let your guard down. It takes a long time to get to know a person; allow yourself that time before you become emotionally and physically attached.

The Bible gives us great advice: "Above all else, guard your heart, for it is the wellspring of life" (Proverbs 4:23).

Sincere Questions

1. **"What if the guy keeps nagging me to have sex with him?"**

Guys who are more interested in your *body* than they are in you will never be satisfied even if you give them what they are asking for. Don't give in to their manipulation. Keep your standards and get rid of the guy. You need a boyfriend who respects you enough to also respect your convictions.

2. **"Girls make me nervous. I'm not interested in sex; I just want to get up enough guts to take a girl to a movie. How do I break the ice?"**

Start a relationship with girls in coed group settings. After you identify a particular girl you'd like to spend an evening with, invite her to a group activity. "Our group is going to the movies Friday night.

Would you like to come with me?" Dating is usually healthiest when done in a group anyway.

3. "I just want to do things together as friends without getting so serious. Is there anything wrong with that?"
Not at all. In fact, you're wise. Often young men and women who are always dating seriously, or "going steady" as it was once called, are insecure, nervous, and possessive. You're not violating any rule of etiquette by simply dating periodically with no strings attached.

4. "Can I date two guys at one time?"
Yes. Just be honest about it with both guys. It's better they learn about it from you than from someone else. If one of the guys gets angry, it's likely he wanted more of a commitment from you than you were ready to make. If he gets angry, that's his problem, not yours.

5. "I've been dating a guy for two and a half years, and lately all we do is fight."
This is a good indication that the relationship is unhealthy. If you can't work out your differences, most likely you need to make the decision to start dating other people.

6. "I've never gone out on a date and I don't want to."

No problem. You're not weird. . .but most likely you'll change your mind someday.

7. "I'd like to date, but I'm just soooo shy!"

Hey, there's probably a girl who looks at you every day at school and says to herself, "Man, I'd love to have a date with him. I wish someone would introduce us. . .but I'm just soooo shy!" Fifty percent of all people are shy, and most of them are also waiting for a date. Just do it.

8. "I like my girlfriend, but her parents drive me crazy."

First of all, maybe you should consider the fact that you may bug her parents, too. In any event, it's tough to show respect for a girl without showing respect for her parents. This doesn't mean parents are perfect. Some parents are difficult to respect. But we need to respect their positions as parents. Parents don't need to do anything to earn our respect. They've already done the one thing that warrants all the respect necessary. They brought us into the world. Since we owe our existence to them, we should respect their position in our lives.

Summary

When you're with a member of the opposite sex, you always want to show respect and consideration. No one wants to be around someone who thinks only of himself or herself. Look out for each other and find ways to make your date happy. Be creative. And whatever you do, always stick to your moral standards, even if it costs you your date.

manners matter manners matter manners manners matter manners manners matter manners matter manners manners matter manners matter manners manners matter manners matter manners

PROM **night**

No doubt about it, prom night is one of the biggest events of the school year. You can't fly by the seat of your pants on this one. Prom night requires more planning and preparation than almost any other social event you'll attend.

Your Date

Of all the decisions you face regarding prom night, without question the biggest decision is this: "Who will I go with?" Choose someone you know will be fun and a good companion for the evening. Choose someone you want to get to know better. Choose someone you respect. Most important, choose someone you trust.

This may seem easier for the guy because in most cases they do the choosing. But girls have the choice to say yes or no. Don't say yes just to ensure a date to prom. It's much better to say no if you doubt his motives or character.

Make sure you give your date plenty of time to plan—four to six weeks ahead of time. If you turn down a date, do so promptly and graciously. The person who asked needs time to make other arrangements.

Your Budget

Prom can be expensive, even if you and your date share expenses. Communicate beforehand who will pay for what. It's standard for the guy to cover the cost of admission to prom (sometimes this is free) and also pay for dinner. Girls, it's thoughtful to offer to pay for the pictures (let's face it, girls care more about pictures anyway.) Guys, plan to buy a corsage for your date; girls, get a boutonniere for yours.

Color Scheme for Attire

It's usually best for the girl to make this choice. Guys, you can match your vest or cummerbund and bow tie with the color of her dress if you choose. Matching isn't necessary, especially if the girl is wearing bright pink. Of course, the standard tuxedo color is black. (Unless you decide to dress like Jim Carrey in *The Mask*, and in that case you should definitely ask your date.) If you don't know what color your date is wearing, it's safe to wear black, silver, or gold accessories.

Flowers

Again, flowers must coordinate with the girl's gown. Guys, it's a good idea to ask your date the color of her dress so you can plan the color of her corsage. White is always a good choice if you're uncertain.

Transportation

If you decide to go to prom with a large group, you may decide to rent a limousine. Make reservations well in advance; prom time can be a busy time for limo services. Be courteous and respectful of the limo driver and the vehicle. Also be prepared to tip at the end of the evening.

Pre-prom

Restaurant

Whichever restaurant you choose, make your selection as early as possible and *make reservations*. Many schools schedule prom on the same night. If this is the case, you may find yourself waiting in a long line outside a restaurant. (Guys, this will be no fun for your date if she's wearing high heels and a sleeveless dress in the middle of January.) Plan ahead. Doing so shows forethought and consideration. (And your date will be impressed.)

Prom Table

Many proms feature tables set up around a large ballroom, with the tables seating four to five couples. It would be smart to preselect your table so you can be sure to have friends seated with you.

Post-prom Party

Next to choosing your date, where you end up following the prom is the second most significant choice you'll make. You need to take into consideration where you and your date's friends are going and what you will be doing. If you don't feel comfortable with the options, plan your own party. Again, start planning as early as possible. *Both you and your date should agree on this important choice.*

Sticking to Your Standards

Prom night is often the most notorious when it comes to drug and alcohol use. If you choose to go to a party where you suspect these activities will take place, decide beforehand, along with your date, that you'll go there to have a great time but you won't drink alcohol or do drugs. If you find yourself at a party that has gotten out of control and you feel it's time to leave, go right away. Your date should always respect your decision.

Remember. . .

All of the other manners we discussed in chapter 9, "Dating Manners," apply **doubly** when you're at prom.

- *Guys:* Choose your date well in advance; ask her parents' permission.

- Be sure you discuss where you'll be going and what you'll be doing the entire night so there will be no surprises.

- *Guys:* Open doors.

- *Guys:* At the table, pull out the chair to seat your date.

- Enjoy conversation. Get to know your date.

- Maintain strict moral standards, no matter how late at night it is.

- Remember your table manners and the principles for effective introductions and meaningful conversation.

- Most important, relax! Enjoy your date and have fun!

Chapter 11

manners matter manners matter manners
matter manners matter manners
matter manners matter
manners
matter
manners
matter

manners
matter manners matter manners matter
manners matter manners matter manners
matter

FAMILY manners

Manners begin at home. If we use our manners around everyone else in our lives but neglect to use them at home, we are phonies. Sure, we can be sloppy and get irritated at home sometimes, but we never want to lose respect for those closest to us.

Time spent at home should be an escape from daily pressures and aggravations. We should all do our share to create a comfortable, peaceful environment where everyone is valued and respected. This may sound a bit idealistic, but let's face it, we all want to be a part of a relaxing home environment. If you can't find this at home, you're probably not going to find it anywhere else.

Courtesy Is Contagious

Simple daily expressions of **politeness** go a **long** way.

- Start every day by greeting everyone. Even a simple "Good morning, Mom" is enough.

- Before you leave for school, wish everyone a good day.

- When you return from school, observe all the nice things your family does for you.

- Say "thank you" for the little things.

  - "Thank you for doing my laundry."

  - "Thank you for fixing my favorite meal. It was delicious."

  - "Thanks for driving me to Sam's house; I had a great time."

  - "Thanks for talking to me about my friends; I'm glad you're interested in my life."

These positive comments may look corny on paper, but they really do make others feel valued and appreciated.

Your **Attitude**

You've heard the saying "Actions speak louder than words." Let's go one step further and say that *attitudes speak louder than actions*. If you don't believe it, just ask your mother after you've emptied the dishwasher while putting on a huge pout-fest and mumbling to yourself about the unfairness of all the work you're expected to do.

We communicate a great deal with our eyes, our expressions, and our tone of voice. If we're angry, frustrated, bored, or offended, it will be obvious to those who know us best—our parents, brothers, and sisters.

Communicating your feelings and being honest about your attitude is the best way to overcome frustration in this area. If your attitude is wrong, ask yourself *why*. Instead of taking it out on your family, pouting, or withdrawing, use words to express what you're feeling. For example:

- "I know you need me to empty the dishwasher tonight, but do you mind if I make a quick phone call first?"

- "I know everyone else wants to eat pizza tonight, but I just had it for lunch; can we agree on something else?"

- "I'm frustrated because I asked you to get out of the shower ten minutes ago and now I'm going to be late."

- "When you laughed at my new haircut, I was hurt."

Making your feelings known will help you express yourself without showing anger or frustration.

Honesty—
Always the Best Policy

All communication is based on **truth** and **accuracy**. The only way a relationship will last is through **trust** and **integrity**. If one family member ceases to be honest, the family begins to break down.

Lies are **born** in a variety of **situations**:

- when we want to seem better than we really are

- when we want to avoid getting in trouble

- when we want to get our own way

- when we're afraid of how people will respond to us if we tell the truth

When parents become suspicious of teenagers, trust begins to break down. "Little white lies" often grow to become even bigger lies. The fact is, no matter what size or color, lying is always lying and it has the same effect as sin—it kills. Lying kills relationships. Lying kills trust.

We must realize that the toughest truth is never as fearful an enemy as the softest lie. We must make a commitment: "I will always tell the truth to my family members—even to my parents—and even when it hurts."

You can fool some of the people all the time, and you can fool all the people some of the time, but you can't fool all the people all the time; and you can't fool God any of the time.

Brothers and Sisters

We often spend more time with brothers and sisters than with anyone else. This overexposure may cause problems. The following guidelines might solve some of your disagreements.

- Give each other space. Respect each other's privacy.

- Don't enter each other's rooms without knocking.

- Don't tease each other.

- Don't tattle on each other. Talk about the problem together first.

- Only borrow with permission and then return promptly.

- Lend freely—especially if you intend to borrow.

- Be protective of one another. Older brothers and sisters should be protective of younger siblings, both physically and morally.

If you and your brother or sister are in the **habit of fighting** with each other, **sit down together and talk** about the sources of conflict.

- clothes

- TV

- music

- bathroom time

- telephone time

- chores

- friends

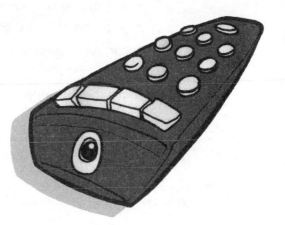

Discuss what you can do about each conflict area to avoid quarreling. If you can't settle an area, ask your parents for their advice.

Family Matters

- •Be respectful of all privileges. . .
  - • time in the bathroom
  - • time in the shower
    - • time on the telephone or Internet
    - • the volume of your stereo
    - • your choice of TV shows
    - • your use of games, computer equipment, etc.

- Always knock before entering anyone else's bedroom or bathroom.

- Keep a confidence—families share secrets that don't need to be broadcast outside the home.

- Give preference to anyone in the family who is sick. Show compassion and kindness.

- Express appreciation. It's easy to get into a rut and take each other for granted. Don't let it happen. Learn to give sincere compliments.

- Give undivided attention. Be a good listener.

- Use table manners even when it's just family.

- Never interrupt someone's conversation unless it's an emergency.

- Clean up after yourself in the bathroom. Rehang towels, dry the floor if it's wet, put away the tooth paste, etc.

- Use air freshener if necessary.

- Take care of your own room by keeping it neat and making your bed each morning.

Habits to Avoid

We develop many habits that in themselves are harmless. However, when observed daily, they tend to drive other people insane—especially people in our own families. Here are a few examples of habits to avoid.

- making bodily noises outside of the bathroom

- cracking your knuckles

- staring

- picking your nose

- picking your teeth

- chewing gum with your mouth open

- vibrating your foot or bouncing your leg up and down nervously

- spitting

Remembering
Important
Dates

When it comes to honoring your family, **remember these** five big days of the year:

- **Christmas:** thoughtful (but not necessarily expensive) gifts for everyone in your immediate family (Mom, Dad, brothers, sisters, and grandparents) purchased with your own money

- **Birthdays:** cards for everyone in your immediate family and gifts for Mom and Dad, brothers and sisters

- **Mother's Day:** card and gift

- **Father's Day:** card and gift

- **Parents' anniversary:** card

*These are the days on which we show honor to the most important people in our lives. Do whatever it takes to remember them!

Chores

While chores are difficult and annoying at times, they do have positive outcomes:

- They teach responsibility.

- They spread the workload around.

- They prepare you to care for yourself—and to care for others.

- They make you more grateful for all the chores your parents do for you every day.

Every teenager **wants** privileges, but with each privilege comes **responsibility**. Chores done efficiently and **without** complaint often serve to **convince** parents that you're ready to be given more **independence**.

It's important for every family member to be a contributing family member. Like players on a team, each member must **pull** together so the whole team functions **well**.

To Do:
1. Trash
2. Vacuum
3. Clean BR
4. Wash Car
5. Laundry
6. Mail Letters
7. Paint Fence
8.
9.

Representatives

When we are outside our home, we represent our family. We want people to think highly of our parents, and therefore we always want to act in a way that reflects positively on them.

In this sense, all manners are family manners. We learn within the home the things we're to practice outside the home. As we learn to practice respect toward our own family members, we'll find it's much easier to show respect toward new acquaintances. In fact, if we're successful at showing honor to our parents and immediate family, we'll be far more likely to be successful throughout our lives.

Children, obey your parents in the Lord, for this is right. "Honor your father and mother"—which is the first commandment with a promise—"that it may go well with you and that you may enjoy long life on the earth."
EPHESIANS 6:1–3

Three Big Words

Three of the most important
words we need to be able to say
within our own families are

"I am sorry."

We all make mistakes. We forget instructions. We
do things that are wrong. Whether we offend our
parents or a brother or sister, when we're wrong
we need to admit our error and assume the blame.
Rather than trying to defend ourselves, make up
excuses, or blame someone else, we should simply
admit our mistakes.

Three More Big Words

Three other words sometimes make us feel awkward, but they're the most important words we can ever say. Parents need to hear them periodically, and even though they may not admit it, brothers and sisters like to hear them, too:

"I love you!"

Dear friends, let us love one another,
for love comes from God.
Everyone who loves has been
born of God and knows God.
1 John 4:7

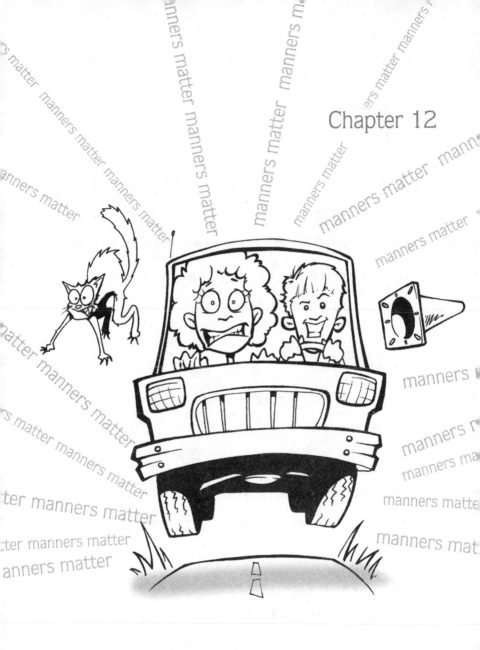

Chapter 12

CAR manners

It's surprising what happens to people when they get behind the wheel of a car. Even the most courteous model citizen can become inconsiderate, aggressive, and dangerous on the road.

It's one thing to mess up and embarrass yourself in public. It's something else to mess up on the highways and risk physical harm or even death. We've learned the importance of respecting people. Now we must learn to respect the two-ton machines we drive every day. Whether you're a driver or a passenger, this chapter is for you.

Good Manners = Safety

- Buckle up! Always wear your seat belt no matter how short the trip. Insist that all of your passengers do, as well.

- Keep your eyes on the road and your hands on the steering wheel at all times.

- Don't assume other drivers will do what they're supposed to do.

- Use the horn only for safety—to notify other drivers of your location. Never use the horn to vent anger.

- You should be in control not only of your car but also of your passengers. If they're a distraction, tell them they can behave or find another ride.

- If you must use your cell phone while driving, make sure you're not in heavy traffic. Maintain a slower speed and never take your eyes off the road.

- This goes without saying, but obey all traffic regulations.

If you are driving, make sure all of your attention is devoted to that task. This is not the time for

- putting on makeup;
- eating;
- drinking coffee;
- organizing CDs; or
- using your cell phone simply to chat with someone.

If you must do these things, pull off the road to a safe spot.

Passenger Manners

When you ride in someone else's car, be sure to show your appreciation for their hospitality, especially if they went out of the way to pick you up. Behave like a good guest.
When you enter the car, be sure to do the following:

- Greet everyone with a smile.

- Say hello, using their names. If you don't know someone, introduce yourself!

- Fasten your seat belt.

- Remain cheerful and cooperative.

When the ride is over, **remember to thank** the driver.

NEVER RIDE WITH STRANGERS!
NEVER GIVE RIDES TO STRANGERS!

Good manners help us to be good passengers with people we know. Good sense tells us *not* to be passengers with people we don't know. It's one thing to ride with a bad driver; it's worse to ride with a bad person.

Never assume that because someone *looks* trustworthy, they *are* trustworthy. The risks are too great.

Road Trips

Spending a great deal of time in a very small space with the same group of people is a test for anyone's manners. Whether you're traveling with your own family or with a friend, you'll find these guidelines helpful:

• Take minimum luggage.

• Bring entertainment: a good book, handheld games, music and headphones, crossword puzzles, etc. But don't use these things while others want to talk with you.

• Bring snack food—enough to share with all passengers. Be sure to ask the driver for permission to eat in the car.

• If the driver gives permission to snack in the car, make every effort not to spill.

• Bring enough money for the trip.

• Participate in meaningful conver.sation.

• Keep your arms and legs in your allotted space.

• Be sure to use the bathroom before leaving. If you must stop at a restroom, say, "I'm sorry, but I need to use a restroom, please."

• Volunteer to help with directions. Help read road signs.

• Offer to share in the gasoline expenses.

• Always thank the driver for the ride.

A car trip is very much like every other part of life's highway. It usually turns out the way we make it.

Getting Your Own Car

Getting our first car is a milestone we all look forward to. Of course, we'd like to have the nicest, newest, fastest car we can get our hands on, but most students have a budget to consider.

- If you'll be paying for gas, mileage per gallon is a very important factor.
- If you're paying for insurance, remember that the more expensive the car, the more expensive the insurance. Also, sports cars are far more expensive to insure.

If you're shopping for a used car, take someone with you who knows what to look for under the hood.

Even if your parents agree to help you purchase a car, it's your responsibility to keep it running well and keep it clean.

- Read the automobile owner's manual. You don't need to be an expert, but it's important to have a general knowledge of your car.
- Make sure you know how to change a tire. (Yes, girls—you, too!) If you've never done it before, practice in your driveway or garage. If your tire ever goes flat on the road, you'll be relieved and prepared.
- Carry a pair of jumper cables in your car in case your battery is dead. They're simple to use and they can

save you a great deal of frustration. This is also a help-ful way to serve others in their need. Warning: Check the owner's manual first; using jumper cables can se-verely damage the computer module in some vehicles.

- Know how to check the fluid levels in your car, including. . .
  - gas
  - oil
  - transmission fluid
  - radiator antifreeze/coolant
  - water in battery
  - washer fluid
  - brake fluid
- Check the air pressure in your tires once a month, and make sure they have proper tread.
- Keep a cell phone with you, if possible. Cell phones provide good security, especially for girls driving at night. In case of an accident or mechanical problem, they provide immediate access to a familiar voice.
- Keep your car clean inside and out, especially the windows, mirrors, and headlights. Each time you come home from a drive, remove all garbage, books, shoes, sports clothes, etc.; don't let the clutter pile up.
- Always buckle up and insist that all passengers use their seat belts. Don't drive on the road until all have cooperated.

Driving Responsibly

Remember: A driver's license is not a right to demand just because you are the legal age; it is a privilege to be earned when you show yourself responsible. A car is potentially a lethal weapon. Every year high school students are killed in auto accidents. Certainly not all fatalities are the fault of teenagers, but some are.

No matter how many times you've seen this list before, read it carefully.

- **Don't drink and drive.** Never allow yourself to be driven by a drunk driver.

- **Don't drive late at night if you're exhausted.** If you find yourself dozing off at the wheel, pull over in a safe area and walk around or get some caffeine. Resume driving when you are more alert.

- **Don't speed for "fun."** Speed limits save lives. Most traffic fatalities are caused by excessive speed. Even driving fast for short distances can cause serious accidents.

- **Don't overload your car.** Make sure there is a seat belt for every passenger.

- **Keep both hands on the wheel**.

- As we've said already, **always wear your seat belt.**

*Driving is a great privilege. Do it responsibly.

186

manners matter   manners matte manners

YOU AND your job

Being a teenager is expensive. Most parents—even though they love you—can't afford to buy you everything you want. An iPod, a new pair of jeans, gas money—these things are costly. Sometimes the only way to afford these expenses is for you to get a job. The idea of hunting for a job might sound daunting, but having a job can actually be a lot of fun if you find something you like to do. It's also invaluable when it comes to teaching you responsibility and discipline and giving you experience that will benefit your future.

Where Do You Start Looking?

- Make a list of things you like to do or places you would like to work.
- Take your list and look on the Internet or in the local newspaper to see what's available.
- Your high school may post job opportunities. Talk to your school guidance counselor.
- If you know a bookstore, coffee shop, or clothing store where you would like to work, make a visit and ask if they are hiring. If they are, ask for an application. Don't be shy—ask to speak to the manager if he or she is in the store. Introduce yourself briefly and tell him or her that you're interested in the position.
- Keep your eyes open for signs advertising "Help Wanted."
- Spread the word. Tell friends and neighbors about your interests. Many times they will have contacts or advice that will help you.

Job Alternatives

You don't have to be employed by someone to make money. If you're creative, you can start your own small business without too much work.

- If you enjoy pets and exercise, start a dog-walking business after school. Offer to take care of pets while owners are away. You'd be surprised how many families go out of town and need someone to watch their pet. You can make flyers or just begin by telling people you know. Determine a reasonable rate to charge, and you're well on your way!

- If you enjoy being with children, make a babysitting flyer with your name and phone number. Post the flyer in your church foyer or place an ad in your community newspaper. Also mention that you are available to house-sit for people who leave town. You'll be surprised how many people will pay good money for someone they know to stay in their home while they are away.

- Start a lawn care business. Create a short newspaper ad that says something like this: "Yard Work: Conscientious high school senior will do anything you need. Call Andrew at [phone number]." If this doesn't promote business, you can deliver flyers to homes in your neighborhood. If the family is home, knock on the door, introduce yourself, and tell them of your lawn care service. They'll be much more likely to ask for your business once they have met you. If your neighbor isn't home, go back another day or leave the flyer by the door.

- If you enjoy baking, start a cake-decorating business.

- Good at math? Begin a tutoring business at a local elementary or middle school.

WARNING!

Getting a job while you're a student can pose a danger. Your job can become time-consuming and begin to take your focus off the importance of finishing school, spending time with your family, going to church, and making good grades. **It's important to make sure your job doesn't distract you** from the things that are most significant in life. If you find this is happening to you, talk to your boss and limit your working hours. You may even need to quit your job, and that's okay.

Take Initiative

Perhaps you're interested in a special field of work. You might select a few companies in that field and write a letter such as this:

52 Main Street
Miami, FL 33901
March 12, 2007

Mr. Douglas Sherlock
Palm Fronds, Inc.
84 Beech Avenue
Miami, FL 33901

Dear Mr. Sherlock:

On June 1 I will be completing my junior year at Miami High School. I am 17 years old and I am preparing for a career as a corporate secretary. My scholastic average is A-. I am very interested in working for your company as a secretary doing any kind of work. I type 58 words a minute without errors.

I would appreciate the privilege of an interview with you. I am available any weekday after 3:30 p.m. My telephone number is (555) 555-5588.

Respectfully,
(Signature)

Jane Smart

*Be sure to type the letter without errors!

192

Creating a Résumé

If you have any job experience, a résumé is helpful.
Keep all information typed on a single sheet of paper.

Name
Address
Home phone number
Education
Elementary school
High school
(Grade point average)
Job Experience
(Most recent listed first)
Job title and explanation of
duties performed
Interests/Achievements
Honors
Awards
Athletics
Career goals
Personal References
1. Teacher
Address
Phone number
2. Family friend
Address
Phone number

The Job Interview

All of the manners we have learned and practiced will pay off during the job interview.

- Arrive at least 15 minutes prior to your appointment.

- Dress appropriately—nothing flashy, but clean and neat. Remember, first impressions count!

- Smile.

- Use the interviewer's title (Mr., Mrs., Ms.) until you are invited to use their first name. If you don't know a woman's marital status, use "Ms."

- Maintain good eye contact.

- Answer questions directly. Be brief and accurate.

- Don't smoke or chew gum during the interview.

- Immediately after the interview, send a brief, personal follow-up letter expressing your appreciation for the opportunity to apply for the job. That follow-up letter might be just the edge you need to secure the position.

You're Hired!

Even after securing the job, you need to maintain good rapport with your boss and those you work with. It's important to be a good employee no matter how small or insignificant the job might seem. Here are some helpful guidelines to keep in mind.

- Be loyal—only speak positively about your boss both inside and outside your job.

- Be kind—not only to those above you on the job, but also to those who work alongside you or even under you.

- Be punctual—arrive at least five minutes earlier than necessary.

- Be enthusiastic. Don't simply do the minimum; do more than is expected.

- Be humble. Be open to criticism and correction. In fact, it's best to solicit honest criticism. Ask your boss, "Sir/Ma'am, I want to serve you to the best of my potential. If you see anything in my performance that needs improvement, I sincerely want you to let me know."

- Never steal items from work. Certainly don't steal time.

*Remember:

An honest day's pay for an honest day's work.

- If you don't understand an assignment, it's your responsibility to ask intelligent questions so you'll be able to do a good job. If you don't ask questions and you fail to complete the assignment, it's your fault.

- Most important, listen carefully. Even if you don't like your boss, listen carefully to all assignments.

- Most jobs require teamwork, so get along well with your coworkers.

- Say "I'm sorry." We all make mistakes. When you do, admit it and move on.

- Don't ask nosy, personal questions. This communicates pride and manipulation. We should be modest and expect the same of others.

- Speak clearly. This communicates mental alertness and accuracy.

Babysitting

Babysitting is not only one of the most common jobs but also one of the most important jobs in the whole world. When you are asked to babysit, you're paid more than a fee—you're paid a compliment! Parents are trusting you with their most valuable possession—their children.

Parents may not say these words, but when they ask you to babysit, they're telling you, *"You're honest, trustworthy, capable, resourceful, loving, responsible, and dependable."* Although babysitting may be a common request, you must never take it lightly. **It is a special trust.**

Before Parents Leave

1. Allergies? Medications?
2. Restrictions? Can the children play outside? Watch TV? Have a snack?
3. Bedtime?
4. Assignments? Homework? Chores?
5. Infant's special needs: Bottle? Diapers?
6. Where are parents going? Name, address, phone number?
7. In case of emergency: Street address, 911, doctor?
8. Answer the phone or let messages go on the answering machine?
9. Receive special permission to use the phone, have a friend over, eat food, or drink a beverage.
10. What time will parents return?

After Parents Leave

1. Care effectively for the children. Be aware of where the children are and what they are doing at all times (especially younger children).
2. Keep the home clean; pick up toys.
3. Do any dishes; empty the dishwasher.
4. Honor the parents' restrictions, including the children's bedtime. If a child stubbornly refuses to obey the curfew, don't use physical discipline and don't allow yourself to become angry. If the child doesn't cooperate with your instructions, simply report the bad behavior to the parents when they return. It's the children's responsibility to obey the babysitter. It's the babysitter's responsibility to tell the parents when they don't.

When Parents Arrive Home

1. Greet them with a smile and ask, "Did you have a good time?"
2. Report any phone calls.
3. Report the children's behavior and bedtime.
4. Thank parents for the opportunity and for their trust.

Babysitting Fee

The fee for babysitting is usually based on an hourly rate and differs according to the number of children, the age of the babysitter, and other demands.

- Always settle the rate prior to the babysitting assignment so that neither you nor the parent will be disappointed.

- Also understand who provides transportation and the hours your service is required. You want to avoid surprises.

manner manners matter manners matter
manners matter manners matter
manners matter manners matter
manners matter manners matter
manners matter manners matter
manners matter manners matter
manners matter manners matter
matter manners matter
matter manners matter
ter manners matter
manners matter
nners matter
ers matter
s matter
matter
er

Chapter 14

LETTER writing

It may seem old-fashioned, but people still experience an unmatched care and excitement when it comes to giving and receiving a handwritten letter that can be read and reread. A telephone call is nice; an e-mail is appropriate for some occasions; but if you want to communicate intimately and genuinely, a letter is the best way to go. Let's face it, you can print out an e-mail, but you would never stand there smelling it or admire the ink and penmanship for years to come.

This chapter will give you some helpful hints about the art of writing letters. (See the next chapter for e-mail etiquette.)

Varieties of Letters

- letters of friendship
- letters of thanks for gifts and special acts of kindness
- letters of appeal
- letters of recommendation
- letters of congratulations
- letters of condolence
- letters for business

Some letters are more **serious** and businesslike.
Some are more **personal.**

When Are Letters Appropriate?

- Whenever gifts are received, a note should be hand-written within one week.

- When family members celebrate birthdays or anniversaries, a card or note of congratulations should be sent.

- When someone has done a special service for us, our appreciation should be expressed in writing. (A friend takes you along on spring break or helps you study for a big test; your brother washes your car; a teacher gives you the opportunity to pull up your grade; and so on.)

- When someone close to us achieves a level of success, a letter of encouragement is always fitting.

- When someone close to us suffers a severe loss, such as a death in the family, a letter of condolence is appropriate. It doesn't have to be long, just sincere.

This last kind of letter isn't easy to write, because we're all inclined to avoid tough subjects. We feel that our attempts to express ourselves might seem awkward or inadequate. Take care that what you say doesn't come out sounding insensitive by mistake.

Again, **manners come to our rescue.** The act of showing **compassion, friendship,** and **love** speaks much louder than our words. Don't spend time **worrying** over *how* to do it—just *do* it! What you say may be just the dose of **encouragement** your friend needs at that time.

Something simple is best at difficult times.

- "I'm so sorry for your loss."

- "I know you will miss your loved one terribly." (If you knew the person who died you can add that you will miss them, too, or say something you liked or will really miss about him or her.)

- "I will pray for you and your family."

- "Is there anything I can do to help you?"

- Never try to point out an "upside" to a person's death. Saying, "Well, at least he isn't in pain anymore," or "It was God's will," won't make your friend feel any less sad and actually might hurt their feelings despite your good intentions.

Surprise Letters

- Whenever you think to yourself, *Boy, I sure am glad to have him/her as a friend,* write that person a short personal note telling them why you appreciate and value them. Spontaneous letters are the best surprises!

- After eating a delicious dinner at a friend's house, write the cook a short note of thanks. Most likely you'll be invited back!

- After attending a really fun party, write the host and tell them how much fun you had.

- After a job interview, take the time to personally thank those who conducted your interview. This may be the edge you need to score the job.

Letter-Writing Necessities

- *Stationery.* While it's not always necessary to use fancy paper to write a letter, it's nice to have on hand some personalized or decorative paper to write those special letters. You don't have to spend much money either; any drugstore or superstore will have many kinds to choose from.

• *Ink.* Never use a pencil to write a letter. Pencil tends to fade and smear easily. Ink is much easier to read and comes in many colors. You can use a unique color to show off your personality when writing. Of course, more serious letters should always be written in black or blue ink.

• *Envelopes.* If you buy stationery, make sure that envelopes are included. If they're not, be sure to buy the right size to fit the card or paper. A small envelope may force you to fold the paper too many times, which ends up looking sloppy.

• *Stamps.* You can always spend extra time picking out interesting stamps at the post office, too. (Now you even have the option of printing your own stamps using a digital picture on your computer!)

• *Return address.* Always be sure to include your return address in the upper left corner or on the back flap of your envelope.

Other Guidelines

- If your letter contains more than a single page, begin the second page on another sheet of paper and number the second and all additional pages.

- If the letter is written to a personal friend or family member for nonbusiness purposes, it should be hand-written.

- If it is for business purposes or to someone outside your family or circle of friends, it should be typed.

- If it is handwritten, it can be written front and back after the first page. The first sheet should always be written only on the front side.

- If you have printed stationery with personal-ized letterhead, the first sheet should always have the letterhead. All other sheets within the letter should be without letterhead.

WARNING!

Whatever you put in writing may be read and reread by more than the single intended recipient. When writing a complaint letter, be courteous in expressing yourself—especially if you are complaining about someone you know. There is also the potential of a love letter ending up in the wrong hands. Be careful not to put on paper things you may regret someday. Finally, avoid gossip. God hates it and it only gets us in trouble.

The Standard Letter

(handwritten)

Date (optional)

Dear Lucy,

Last week was the highlight of my summer. Thank you for inviting me to Florida with your family. It was everything you told me about and more—especially the snorkeling. Now I just hope to recover from my jellyfish sting! You are a wonderful friend and I'm so glad we can laugh together about everything! Maybe next time we can meet some lifeguards!

Much love (or whichever closing you choose),

Your signature

The Formal Letter

(typed)

Your name
Your address
Date

Their name
Their address

Dear Mr. Maui,

I appreciate the free trip you gave me to Hawaii last month. That was most generous. I enjoyed feeding your gerbil while you were out of town for the weekend. I would be happy to serve you again.

Most sincerely,

Your signature

Your name (typed)

Remember...

- Use proper margins on both sides.

- Use whichever closing you choose.

- Sign your name above your typed name.

Thank-You Notes

If we're not thankful for what we've got, we're not likely to be thankful for what we're going to get. In other words, if we don't express thanks for a gift we receive, we may not receive gifts in the future. It's much more fun to give to grateful people!

We all receive **special gifts of love** that deserve a special response:

- a Christmas or birthday gift from someone out of state or across town
- a money gift or other gift sent through the mail
- a special favor
- an overnight visit
- a dinner party or luncheon
- a special event

You may be overwhelmed on certain occasions (such as your birthday or graduation) when you have a long list of people you need to thank. Remember that your note of thanks can be *brief*. But it also should be *sincere*. Don't give in to the temptation to write the same words of thanks in every note you send; always make each note personal, remembering to mention the gift you received, how you plan to use it, how much you appreciate it, etc.

*Thank-you notes are available at almost any store, but don't let that stop you from creating your own for a personal touch. Simply fold a plain piece of paper both ways and use your creativity to make it look special.

211

Sample Thank-You Note

(handwritten)

Date

Dear Grandma and Grandpa,

It was so thoughtful of you to give me a brand-new BMW for my graduation. Red is my favorite color. I will take good care of it.

You are special to me.

Love,
Fred

P.S. My friends like the car, too.

Summary

- Personal letters or notes should be handwritten.

- Business or formal letters should be typed, using proper margins and proper spacing.

- Thank-you notes should be sent within one week after a gift is received.

- Whatever you put in writing may be read and reread by people other than the intended recipient. Be careful what you write—it might come back and embarrass you if you're not careful.

*Send a thank-you note to a friend this week. Tell them what you admire about them and how much you appreciate their friendship.

Chapter 15

E-MAIL *etiquette*

E-mail is one of the most convenient and widely used ways to communicate today (perhaps second only to the cell phone). Although the Internet may be complex technology for some of us, the rules of etiquette still apply. Basic courtesy is expected—meaning that you should treat others the way you want to be treated.

The rules of Internet etiquette, or "netiquette" as it is often called, may be common sense to some of you, but several rules may require some practice.

Addressing an E-mail

- Be sure to address the e-mail *only* to the intended recipient.

- When responding to a previously sent e-mail, be sure not to "reply to all" unless your e-mail pertains to the entire group.

- Be sure to fill in the subject line of your e-mail before you send it, even if you only type the word "hi."

Writing an E-mail

Remember that the recipient of your e-mail can't hear your tone of voice or see your face when they read your message. It's important to make your words clear. When all you have is a keyboard to convey your thoughts, you'd better use it carefully!

- Always begin your e-mail with a short greeting. You would never call someone on the phone and begin by asking them for a favor before saying "hello." The same principle applies to e-mail.

- Don't use all UPPERCASE letters when writing an e-mail. This comes across as shouting. Unless your message is very urgent, you should use capital and lowercase letters just as you would in a normal document.

- Be brief. If you have a lot to say, save yourself (and the other person) the time and call them on the phone.

- Important or personal information should not be conveyed through e-mail. It's always best to speak face-to-face or over the telephone when you have important news for someone.

- Don't gossip. E-mails can easily be forwarded to people we don't intend.

- If you're afraid something you've written could possibly offend someone, delete it or rephrase it.

- Before you click SEND, reread your e-mail and check for spelling or grammar mistakes.

Responding to E-mail

As with returning a phone call, we are expected to respond to e-mails in a timely manner, especially when a friend has written to ask you a question or you have received an electronic invitation (E-vite) to a party. It's polite to respond promptly. Junk mail can be ignored, but you should always respond to a real message.

If you don't check your e-mail very often, let people know so they don't expect an immediate reply. If you plan to be away from your computer for a period of time, use the "vacation" or "auto-reply" feature, which automatically lets the sender know their message was received and when to expect your reply.

Sending
and
Receiving
Attachments

Don't send attached files unless you know the recipient can open them in a timely manner. Not everyone has high-speed Internet access; downloading or opening a large attachment on a computer with dial-up could take several minutes. If you're sending a picture as an attachment, try to make it smaller to increase download speed. Keep your antivirus and antispyware programs current, as well, so you don't send unwanted programs with your attachments.

When you're on the receiving end of an unknown attachment or link, don't open it. The attachment could contain a virus that could crash your computer system or other malicious software such as spyware; links could take you to malicious Web sites.

Forwarding

The **FORWARD** button is a convenient way to spread news or information. It can be helpful in many situations, but it also can be widely overused and abused. The Internet was not intended to be a way to spread jokes, chain letters, or political messages.

- If you receive any annoying messages from unknown addresses, the best thing to do is either report them as spam or delete and ignore them.

- Unless you are sure that someone would benefit (or laugh) from receiving a forwarded message, don't send it.

- Remove the e-mail addresses of previous recipients to protect their privacy, and if you send to multiple recipients, use "blind copy" if your e-mail has that option.

- Think twice before sending or forwarding an e-mail that could be misinterpreted or offensive.

- Don't participate in e-mail gossip. Never forward a personal message that was intended for your eyes only.

Instant Messaging

Instant Messaging has become quite popular with students these days. In many cases, its popularity has taken the common use of the telephone by storm. Using IM is a much more casual and less personal way of communicating, making it less demanding. It is also very convenient, especially for those who can type fast.

But as with any communication in cyberspace, you need to keep some guidelines in mind:

- Always know who you are "chatting" with. Don't respond to an unknown screen name.

- Be careful with your words. There is no guarantee that your words are seen only by the person you are writing to.

- Remember that your words will be sent as soon as you press ENTER or SEND.

- If you don't get a response, don't keep sending messages. Stop until you hear back from that person.

- Respect other people's time. If they say they need to go, honor that.

- If you're using IM at home, be courteous and don't tie up your phone line.

Using Symbols and Abbreviations

Sometimes the thoughts and emotions we intend to convey with our words can be easily misunderstood by the recipient, who can't look at you or hear your voice. It can be helpful to use certain symbols (called "emoticons") to convey emotions when you write e-mails. Abbreviations also can be time-savers when you're sending quick messages. Remember that symbols and abbreviations are to be used when writing *informally*.

Common Symbols
:-)	smile, happy, laugh
:-(	frown, unhappy
;-)	winking, just kidding
:-o	angry, yelling, shocked
:-l	hmm. . .
[[ ]]	hugs
**	kisses

Common Abbreviations
AAK	asleep at keyboard
B4N	bye for now
BTW	by the way
IOW	in other words
LOL	laughing out loud
OTF	on the floor (laughing)
ROTFL	rolling on the floor laughing
TAFN	that's all for now
XOXO	hugs and kisses

*Unlike the telephone and letters, e-mail allows us to be somewhat anonymous when we communicate with people. Of course we have a screen name and an e-mail address that identify us to familiar people, but overall it is a very impersonal, detached way of communicating. This is one reason we should stick to e-mailing our friends and family—people we know and trust.

WARNING!

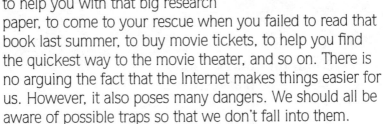

The World Wide Web has opened many doors for us. As a student, you've certainly made friends with the Internet to help you with that big research paper, to come to your rescue when you failed to read that book last summer, to buy movie tickets, to help you find the quickest way to the movie theater, and so on. There is no arguing the fact that the Internet makes things easier for us. However, it also poses many dangers. We should all be aware of possible traps so that we don't fall into them.

Unfortunately, some people use the Internet to pull off things they wouldn't dare try in real life. The news is full of stories about creeps who use the Internet to feed their sinful habits. This is why you must be extremely careful whenever you are online. Here are a few guidelines to follow:

• Consider everyone you meet online a stranger—someone not to be trusted. Strangers include those you've encountered online before; just because you've chatted with them online doesn't make them people you should trust or talk with openly.

• Never give personal information to a stranger.

• Always be careful when entering chat rooms, discussion groups, and other online forums. Your computer leaves traces at every site you visit. If you happen to stumble upon a morally offensive site, there are ways you could be targeted in the future.

• If your family hasn't enabled "pop-up" controls on your computer, talk to them about doing so. Again, keep your antivirus and anti-spyware programs current and use a good firewall to keep hackers out of your computer.

• If you happen to stumble upon a pornographic site or other objectionable site, tell your parents immediately. They will respect you for your honesty and it will save all of you from much pain down the road. Most important, this is what would please the Lord!

• Avoid "Internet dating" or forming a relationship with someone you have never met in person. Remember how easy it is to lie and mislead when you communicate without being seen. This can lead not only to emotional hurt but also to physical danger.

- Limit the time you spend online.

*A good general rule you should commit yourself to when using the computer is this: Always have a purpose when you sit down to use the computer. If you don't have a purpose, it's easy to fall into temptation or become lazy.

I will walk in my house with blameless heart.
I will set before my eyes no vile thing.
PSALM 101:2–3

Chapter 16

BEING A gracious guest

*When you're a guest, bring a **minimum** of gear and a **maximum** of manners.

You may wonder why some people get invited to every fun event. It may have to do with their ability to make others feel comfortable in their presence. We all like to be around fun people. In this chapter you'll learn everything you need to know to be the one who is always invited back.

Many of the same rules we discussed in chapter 11, "Family Manners," apply here. Only it's not our house, so we must be extra careful to be considerate before opening the fridge or turning on the TV. We can still have fun and show respect at the same time.

- Respond promptly to the invitation. If you can't give an answer right away, let them know when you will have a definite answer.

- Stay at home if you're sick. No need to spread your germs.

- As you enter the house, if your shoes are wet or dirty, leave them at the door.

- Remember to smile, make eye contact, and engage in pleasant conversation.

- Interact comfortably with your friend's parents. Use their names. "That's an interesting story, Mr. Snyder."

- Always hang up your clothes or keep them neatly in your bag.

- Always knock before opening closed doors.

- Depend on your host to clue you in on the following:

  - where you will sleep

  - breakfast time

  - curfew

  - any special household rules

- Show appreciation for the hospitality, especially at meals. Verbalize your feelings. "This meat loaf is delicious, Mrs. Cherry!"

- Don't touch anything that may be fragile. You never know which knickknack may have been in the family for centuries.

- Always ask permission to use the phone. (Never call long distance on your host's bill.)

- Keep the bathroom neat.

- Avoid long showers.

- If you use a towel, hang it up to dry.

- Make your bed.

- Be considerate of the noise level—especially when others have gone to bed.

- Volunteer to clean. (Offer to help clean the table after dinner, for example.)

- Don't bring your pet!

*Sending a thank-you note to your host is always a thoughtful gesture, especially if your stay was longer than just one day. You may not have felt as though you were any trouble (after all the rules you worked so hard to follow), but this is just one way to ensure another welcomed visit in the future.

Pool or Hot Tub Manners

It's always fun to swim in a private pool. It's easy to let your excitement get the best of you and your energy to get out of control. This is when accidents can happen. Just remember that even though you are outside and parents may not be watching you, certain rules still apply.

- If you don't know how to swim, don't be embarrassed. Tell an adult and stay in the shallow end.
- Don't run around the pool.
- Don't push people into the pool.
- Don't take food or drink into the pool.
- Be sure you know all the pool rules and obey them.
- Think ahead. The pool is definitely not the bathroom.
- Don't enter the house dripping wet.
- When your swimsuit is wet, don't sit on any furniture except "outdoor furniture."

Pool rules, like all household rules, aren't designed to ruin your fun. They are meant to guarantee a good time by avoiding an accident, a fight, or worse. They're really for everyone's benefit.

So we put our manners into practice and have a great visit. And when friends come to visit us, we appreciate their manners. That's the whole idea behind manners—they work both ways.

manners matter
manners matter man
manners matter ma
manners
matter
matter
manners
ers manners matter
ers matter manners manne
ners manners matter mann
ners matter mann

SCHOOL manners

Despite what many students think, the primary purpose of school is *education*, not entertainment. Of course learning should be exciting and even fun. But it's important as we grow up to learn to identify the things that help us mature and the things that don't.

Respect Your Teachers

Your teachers are the authority when you're at school. They're the ones who assign homework and give **grades**, **privileges**, **detentions**, **time-outs**, and—yes—even **graduation diplomas**. Whether you like them or not, they have earned the right to be shown respect.

You don't have to be on the honor roll to understand the importance of good relationships with your teachers.

• Remember that your teachers deserve your respect and attention.

• Greet your teachers each day by name. If they have a title, be sure to use it. "Good morning, Dr. Sweetgum."

• Never answer a question by saying "yeah."

• Always use the phrases "Yes, ma'am," "No, ma'am," "Yes, sir," "No, sir."

• Write down all assignments accurately.

• Don't hesitate to ask a question if something isn't clear. Your teachers *want* you to understand.

• Don't just study enough to survive. Study to thrive!

• Don't be reluctant to do more than is expected of you.

Respect Your Classmates

You're **not responsible** *for* your **classmates**, but you are responsible *to* them. This means you should treat them with **kindness** and **sincerity** (as you would want to be treated). It doesn't mean you should try to be best friends with everyone, only that you give compliments and show respect to others rather than criticizing or teasing them.

Obviously, we don't all have the same **looks**, **talents**, or **personalities**, because **God** made each one of us **unique**. That's why it's **ignorant** and **foolish** to **joke** about such **differences** rather than **respect** them. In the same way, you should **never** laugh at classmates when they make **mistakes**.

Strive to be a **positive influence** in your class.

- Become friends with a new student or someone who may be an outsider.

- Be a peacemaker.

- Assist a student who is struggling academically.

- Get involved in your class government to make positive changes in your school.

- Set a good example for your classmates.

Cheating

Cheating is a sneaky habit. It crawls in the back door and does its dirty work without being noticed—usually. That's how cheating starts. **The truth is**, when you cheat, you're not cheating the teacher; **you're cheating yourself.**

Some students give the following reasons to justify their cheating:

- "I'm afraid of failure."

- "I forgot the assignment."

- "Cheating is easier than studying."

- "I'll flunk if I don't cheat!"

It can be easy to become disillusioned and begin to think that cheating is only a slight offense. Cheating, however, is a serious crime. At its root, it is a form of stealing and lying. Cheating establishes a very destructive pattern in your life as you begin to avoid owning responsibility for your actions. It will eventually prevent you from becoming a mature adult.

Cheating is weakness at its worst. In the end, it cheats us of our own abilities.

Enjoy School!

You've heard the saying "This is your life; live it!" You may think that your life begins *after* school, but that's not true. Your life is *now!* A big part of your life right now involves school, so you might as well make the most of it!

- Soak it in. Pay attention. Take notes. Exercise your brain.

- There is a good reason for homework. Do it.

- Don't procrastinate. Work ahead.

- Read. If you don't like to read, chances are you haven't found a good book. Ask a friend or respected teacher for advice. All it takes is one good book to get hooked.

*An education isn't something we've had; it's something we're always getting.

manners matter manners matter manners matter manners matter manners matter manners matter manners matter manners matter manners matter manners matter manners matter manners matter manners matter manners matter manners matter manners matter manners matter manners matter manners matter

CHURCH manners

Manners affect our relationships
with people. Church manners can
affect our relationship with God.
Sounds pretty serious, doesn't it?
At the same time, God wants us to
be comfortable with church. It's His
house and He wants us to feel right
at home. His children should relax and
sense His acceptance. He loves you
and He's the author of manners.

Why Church?

At church you can be **part**

of something **much bigger**

than yourself. God gave

His children **special gifts**

in order to **serve** as **members**

of **the body of Christ**—the

church. As you begin to serve, you

may be **surprised** by the **joy** that

fills your **life** as you become **less**

focused on **yourself** and **more**

focused on **God**.

Do I *Really* Need Church?

It seems that many students today feel that there are better ways to spend their time than going to church. It can feel outdated and useless. But God knows what His children need and He created church in order to help meet those needs. Not only is church a place where we come to meet with Him; it's the place we come to meet with others. In other words, it's the perfect place to practice your manners.

Before Church

- Bring your Bible.

- Leave your cell phone in the car.

- Always make sure you dress appropriately.

- Invite others to come with you.

During the Service

- Don't distract others (and don't sit by those who will distract you).

- Don't talk or pass notes.

- Listen carefully to the message and take notes.

- Actively participate during the service.

After Church

- Don't rush off to lunch; take time to talk with people.

- Find someone who might be visiting and make them feel welcome.

- Ask your friends about their week and the time they spent with God.

"Why do I have to go to church when I can watch it on TV?"

The difference between going to church and watching it on TV is similar to the difference between calling your girlfriend on the phone and actually having a date with her. You will never experience God or truly know Him until you get involved. One of the ways you can do this is through your local church.

Churches offer several **opportunities** to get involved:

- Sunday school
- small groups
- choir
- youth groups
- volunteering in the nursery
- teaching a children's class
- going on mission trips
- praying for others

Being **involved** in a local **church** gives us the **opportunity** to become **more like Christ** by **serving** and **loving** others. **Unfortunately,** not everyone comes to church with a God-centered mind-set.

For example:

- "Kim's wearing the same dress she wore last week."

- "Jim's sitting with Pam again. They just don't seem right for each other."

- "Oh brother! I can't believe we're singing that chorus again!"

Sadly, sometimes we might find that **being in church** is no more **uplifting** than being anywhere else in the world. **Members** of any congregation can **succumb** to the sins of **gossip, self-righteousness**, and much worse— whether they are **in church or not**. **Ridicule** of others and **contempt** for others **don't belong in our lives**, and they certainly **don't belong at church**. Never participate in **negative behavior**, even if you see it happening **in your church**.

Church is not a place to come and critique others. Church is a place to **worship God** and **encourage others**. The Bible reminds us that "the tongue has the power of life and death" (Proverbs 18:21). **Speak words that bring life, not death.**

Christians and **nonbelievers** are equally capable of hurting others with **unkind words** and **actions**, so instead of looking at **church behavior** in terms of **human standards**, let's look at how **God intended** us to act—wherever we are. **He has the best perspective.**

God tells us

- to love each other (1 John 4:7);

- to forgive and help one another (Matthew 18:21–22; Galatians 6:2);

- to turn the other cheek (Matthew 5:39); and

- to go the second mile (Matthew 5:41).

Pretty practical manners, aren't they? It's easy to see what this kind of behavior can do for our relationships—not just at church but in our homes, our schools, and our neighborhoods.

We quickly learn that while church manners show our respect for God, they also do a lot inside our hearts. As we give God the respect He deserves in our lives and show that same respect to others, we begin to experience the highest form of manners—godly character—taking hold of our lives.

The words we sing and pray and read in church begin to take shape in us. Words like these:

- love

- joy

- peace

- patience

- kindness

- goodness

- faithfulness

- gentleness

- self-control

If you're a child of God, He's calling you to something great in this life. And He's calling you to accomplish it with the help of others. Don't miss out on this incredible adventure.

A wise man once said, "Remember your Creator in the days of your youth" (Ecclesiastes 12:1). These are the best days of your life. Use them to accomplish what is most important.

More Important
Than Manners

What? After all we have discussed in this book about manners, is there really something more important? Of course there is! Feeling good about yourself and your relationships with others is important, but it's not **most important.** The truth is, none of the principles in this book matter if you're living your life only for yourself and for the approval of others. **What matters most is having a right relationship with God.**

God created you to know Him, and because of that, you will find fulfillment in life only when you have come into a relationship with Him. If you don't know for sure that you have a personal relationship with Him, **ask Him** to give you that now. **Trust** in the death and resurrection of Jesus Christ to save you from your sin, turn from your sin, and **offer** your life to Him.

Manners matter—but having a relationship with God through Jesus Christ matters more!

Also for teens...

IF YOU'RE TIRED OF HEARING

THE FLUFFY VERSION OF THE HARD ISSUES,

THIS DEVOTIONAL IS FOR YOU.

Price $9.97

ISBN 978-1-59310-489-4

Fifty of the toughest issues you'll ever face are delivered full-force in this powerful devotional from popular youth speaker and author Phil Chalmers. Covering issues like sex, suicide, the media, abortion, violence—and much more—you'll discover that yeah, life IS hard...

But it doesn't have to be **THAT HARD!**

Chalmers unveils the truth behind the issues and offers real solutions for real problems—**for real people just like you.**

So what are you waiting for? Break open this book and discover the truth—**if you can handle it!**

Available wherever Christian books are sold